FIRST DECREES OF SOVIET POWER

FIRST DECREES OF SOVIET POWER

compiled, with introduction and explanatory notes by

YURI AKHAPKIN

1970
Lawrence & Wishart

SBN 853/5 224 1

Printed in Great Britain by
Unwin Brothers Limited
Woking and London

CONTENTS

INTRODUCTION

During the first nine months following the October Revolution, 1917, more than 950 decrees and other enactments are known to have been issued by the first supreme bodies of Soviet power—the All-Russia Central Executive Committee (ARCEC) and the Council of People's Commissars (CPC).

These range from the first Acts proclaiming and affirming the rule of the workers and poorest peasants of Russia, to the first Soviet Constitution.

The legislative activity undertaken in those stormy months, when the foundations were established of the world's first State of workers and peasants, covered all basic aspects of Soviet statehood. The Soviet Government and the Bolshevik Party, now the ruling party, made the principles of their policy known to the millions of ordinary workers and peasants by the mass publication of all decrees and decisions. And the masses of the people, wishing to build their life on new foundations, accepted that policy and gave the Soviets and the Bolsheviks the full confidence without which leadership in the revolutionary movement is impossible.

The very first decrees, on peace and on land, written by Lenin and adopted by the Second All-Russia Congress of Soviets, met the two principal demands of the masses who had carried out the October Revolution: to end the imperialist war, and to hand the land over to the toiling peasantry for use in perpetuity. The Decree on Peace proclaimed the basic principles of the peaceful foreign policy of the Soviet State, and called upon the peoples of all countries to do away with wars once for all. The Decree on Land began the revolutionary transformation of agrarian relationships and created the conditions for gradual transition to socialism in agriculture.

Collected in this book are the most important legislative acts adopted in the first nine months of Soviet power. This legislation began to implement the Bolshevik Party's political and economic programme, worked out before the proletarian revolution.

These acts ensured the destruction of the bourgeois State machinery—the old Ministries, judicature, Army and Navy. They put a stop to the sabotage of the bourgeoisie and reactionary officialdom, and disbanded the counter-revolutionary parties and organizations. At the same time they began the building of the Soviet State apparatus. The first Soviet Government was set up—the Council of People's Commissars, with Lenin at the head. New central executive bodies were formed—People's Commissariats, a new Army, a new judicial system. The power of the Soviets of Workers', Soldiers', Peasants' and Cossacks' Deputies was consolidated, as the political form of the dictatorship of the working class.

In the economic sphere problems of tremendous importance were solved: the entire economic life of the country was reorganized along socialist lines. Priority was given to undermining the economic base of the bourgeoisie. Production and distribution were placed under workers' control; banks, large industrial enterprises and whole economic sectors were nationalized, and on June 28, 1918, nationalization was extended to all basic industries. As a transitional measure in establishing State and public control over the distribution of food and other prime necessities, a decree on consumer co-operatives was issued, placing them under the control of Soviet governmental bodies and of the working people represented in each individual co-operative.

A key role in reorganizing the economy was played by the Supreme Economic Council. Set up on the proposal of Lenin, it led the way in creating a new type of machinery to run the country's economy.

At the same time, the new legislation tackled the problems that the bourgeois-democratic revolution in February 1917 had failed to solve, including the abolition of landed proprietorship, elimination of the division of society into Estates, separation of the Church from the State the placing of women on an equal footing with men in all spheres.

The question of nationalities, very acute in multi-national Russia, was also decided. The Soviet Government decreed and ensured the equality and sovereignty of the peoples of the country; the right of every people to self-determination, including the right to secede and form an independent State; the abolition of all national restrictions; the free development of all nationalities. The main Act formalizing the fundamentals of Soviet policy for the nationalities was the Declaration of Rights of the Peoples of Russia.

Even in conditions of economic dislocation and incipient counter-revolution the Soviet Government constantly concerned itself with the working peoples' well-being. Laws were enacted for the protection of labour in factories and offices, for the regulation of wages, and on unemployment and sickness benefits.

The legislation of the first months established the guidelines for the development of science and culture. Decrees were adopted on the work of the Academy of Sciences in investigating the country's natural resources, on the protection of the Republic's monuments, on the introduction of the West European calendar, and on bringing all educational establishments under the People's Commissariat for Public Education. The latter decree was the first step in reorganizing the system of education and upbringing of the younger generation. It was followed by the approval, on September 30, 1918, of the Statute of the common secondary school, under which instruction in all schools was to be conducted on unified general educational and polytechnical lines, with due attention to physical and aesthetic training. Two months earlier, on August 2, 1918, a decree, with corresponding regulations, had been issued on the preferential admission of workers and poor peasants to higher educational establishments. These two Acts introduced free tuition and student allowances for all citizens of both sexes who had reached the age of sixteen.

Included in this book are the first two Constitutional Acts—the Declaration of Rights of the Working and Exploited People, and the Constitution of the Russian Federation. These gave legal embodiment to everything accomplished under Soviet rule in the first months following the Revolution: the establishment of the new State system based on the Soviets, the abolition of private capitalist and landed proprietorship and of the exploitation of man by man, the provision of equal status of all the peoples inhabiting Russia.

In all this legislative activity Lenin, the Chairman of the Council of People's Commissars, played a vital part. As head of the Soviet Government he guided all aspects of the life of the new Soviet Republic, attending to the most diverse questions of economic management and State administration. He himself was the author of many important decrees, and a number of decrees were edited by him. All were discussed and adopted by the Central Executive Committee and the Council of People's Commissars with his direct participation, and many were placed before them on his initiative.

Much of the credit for oganizing the process of legislation belongs to Lenin. Laws were drafted in the first place by the central executive bodies, or by inter-departmental commissions set up by the Government for the purpose. All the departments concerned either took part in preparing the draft or were obliged, before a draft was submitted to the Government, to study it and introduce whatever amendments they found necessary. The People's Commissariats for Justice, Finance and State Control were always required to examine all draft laws, since without their sanction none could be discussed by the Government. Laws were adopted by a majority vote. Sverdlov, the Chairman of the All-Russia Central Executive Committee, and Lenin, the Chairman of the Council of People's Commissars, had no special privileges as compared with the other members of these bodies. Within two days of their adoption, decrees had to be published in the central Government newspapers—*Izvestia* and *Gazeta Vremennogo Rabochego i Krestyanskogo Pravitelstva*—and in the "Collection of Laws and Ordinances of the Workers' and Peasants' Government".

The strictly businesslike manner in which sittings of the Council of People's Commissars were always conducted is worth recalling. Lenin could so organize and direct work that in meetings of a few hours the Council could manage to decide twenty to thirty questions of great public importance. A. V. Lunarcharsky, People's Commissar for Education, has vividly described the atmosphere at these sittings in his *Reminiscences of V. I. Lenin* (Politizdat, Vol. 3, Moscow, 1969):

> "Things hummed in *Sovnarkom* under Lenin. A definite pattern of procedure was established: extreme stringency in allotting time to speakers, whether our own or *rapporteurs* from outside. Everyone who took the floor had to be very concise and matter-of-fact. A kind of condensed atmosphere prevailed in *Sovnarkom*; time seemed to have thickened, when so many facts, ideas and decisions were packed into every

minute. And yet there was not the faintest smack of officialdom, not a trace of playing at self-importance, not even of the strain of people doing back-breaking work."

Council sittings were opened by Lenin strictly on time, and attendance of all the People's Commissars was obligatory. At the close of each sitting the day and hour of the next were fixed and entered, as a rule, in the minutes. Sittings were opened at 6.00, 7.00 and sometimes 8.00 p.m. A very punctual man himself, Lenin did not tolerate lateness and, according to eyewitnesses, always rebuked latecomers. Sometimes he would do this by scribbling a note and passing it to the offender; several such notes are to be found in Lenin's archives. In one of them, he wrote to People's Commissar for Foreign Affairs, Chicherin: "You are late again".

The Council of People's Commissars could be attended, with a voice but no vote, by board members of the People's Commissariats, but only when questions affecting their Commissariats were being discussed.

Sitting began with discussion of the agenda: it was decided which questions should be examined and which put aside or returned to the respective departments for further elaboration. Lenin insisted on a strict time-limit: five minutes for reports, three for speeches during discussion, and enforced it relentlessly. His archives contain many scraps of paper on which he put down the names of the speakers: against every name is indicated the time of the beginning and end of the speech. Nor did he make any exception for himself. If a speaker did not finish within the time-limit Lenin would always stop him, and perhaps ask two or three questions on the substance of what he had still to say.

The work of the Council of People's Commissars was not kept secret from the people. By its decision of January 5, 1918, the central Government newspapers published not only the texts of decrees and other legislative acts but also reports of the Council's proceedings. These were prepared, under Lenin's supervision, by the CPC Press Bureau, which was set up immediately following the Revolution, and by the Council's secretary.

Most of the enactments published in this book have been taken and translated from the publication *Decrees of the Soviet Government*, volumes 1 and 2, which appeared respectively in 1957 and 1959, prepared by the Institute of Marxism–Leninism of the Central Committee of the Communist Party of the Soviet Union and the Institute of History of the U.S.S.R. Academy of Sciences. This is referred to below as *Decrees*.

All documents are numbered and arranged chronologically.

Documents issued before February 14 (1), 1918, have two dates, the first according to the Gregorian calendar, known as the "West European" or "New Style", the second (printed in brackets) according to the Julian or "Old Style" calendar which was in use in old Russia. The Old Style was abolished and the New Style introduced by the Decree of February 6 (January 24), 1918, signed by Lenin. Documents issued after February 14, 1918, have only New Style dates.

Explanatory notes concerning most of the documents (to which the superior numbers against the titles refer) are included at the end of the book.

It is hoped that this collection will help familiarize English readers with the social essence of the system that triumphed in Russia as a result of the October Revolution. Its contents present a vivid picture of the nature and moral make-up of the new society and of the new State that emerged within the confines of the former Russian empire. Herein lies the historical interest of the Decrees, although many of them were of transient significance. They owed their appearance to the specific conditions of the time, the economic situation in the country, the political and social relationships in Russia, born of the great revolution and destined to develop in grim struggle.

YURY AKHAPKIN, Moscow, 1970

1. "TO THE CITIZENS OF RUSSIA!"—APPEAL OF THE PETROGRAD MILITARY REVOLUTIONARY COMMITTEE[1]

November 7 (October 25), 1917

The Provisional Government has been deposed. State power has passed into the hands of the organ of the Petrograd Soviet of Workers' and Soldiers' Deputies—the Military Revolutionary Committee, which heads the Petrograd proletariat and the garrison.

The cause for which the people have fought, namely, the immediate offer of a democratic peace, the abolition of landed proprietorship, workers' control over production, and the establishment of Soviet power—this cause has been secured.

Long live the revolution of workers, soldiers and peasants!

Military Revolutionary Committee of the Petrograd Soviet of Workers' and Soldiers' Deputies.

10 a.m., October 25, 1917.

Decrees, Vol. 1, p. 2.

2. "TO WORKERS, SOLDIERS AND PEASANTS!" —APPEAL OF THE SECOND ALL-RUSSIA CONGRESS OF SOVIETS IN CONNECTION WITH THE VICTORY OF THE OCTOBER REVOLUTION AND THE TASKS FACING IT[2]

November 7 (October 25), 1917

The Second All-Russia Congress of Soviets of Workers' and Soldiers' Deputies has opened. The vast majority of the Soviets are represented at the Congress. A number of delegates from the Peasants' Soviets are also present. The mandate of the compromising Central Executive Committee has terminated. Backed by the will of the vast majority of the workers, soldiers and peasants, backed by the victorious uprising of the workers and the garrison which has taken place in Petrograd, the Congress takes power into its own hands.

The Provisional Government has been overthrown. The majority of the members of the Provisional Government have already been arrested.

The Soviet Government will propose an immediate democratic peace to all the nations and an immediate armistice on all fronts. It will secure the transfer of the land of the landed proprietors, the crown and the monasteries to the peasant committees without compensation; it will protect the rights of the soldiers by introducing complete democracy in the army; it will establish workers' control over production; it will ensure the convocation of the Constituent Assembly at the time appointed; it will see to it that bread is supplied to the cities and prime necessities to the villages; it will guarantee all the nations inhabiting Russia the genuine right to self-determination.

The Congress decrees: all power in the localities shall pass to the Soviets of Workers', Soldiers' and Peasants' Deputies, which must guarantee genuine revolutionary order.

The Congress calls upon the soldiers in the trenches to be vigilant and firm. The Congress of Soviets is convinced that the revolutionary army will be able to defend the revolution against all attacks of imperialism until such time as the new government succeeds in concluding a democratic peace, which it will propose directly to all peoples. The new government will do everything to fully supply the revolutionary army, by means of a determined policy of requisitions and taxation of the propertied classes, and also will improve the condition of soldiers' families.

The Kornilov men—Kerensky, Kaledin and others—are attempting to bring troops against Petrograd. Several detachments, whom Kerensky had moved by deceiving them, have come over to the side of the insurgent people.

SOLDIERS, ACTIVELY RESIST KERENSKY THE KORNILOVITE! BE ON YOUR GUARD!

RAILWAYMEN, HOLD UP ALL TROOP TRAINS DISPATCHED BY KERENSKY AGAINST PETROGRAD!

SOLDIERS, WORKERS IN FACTORY AND OFFICE, THE FATE OF THE REVOLUTION AND THE FATE OF THE DEMOCRATIC PEACE IS IN YOUR HANDS!

LONG LIVE THE REVOLUTION!

The All-Russia Congress of Soviets of Workers' and Soldiers' Deputies. The Delegates from the Peasants' Soviets.

Decrees, Vol. 1, pp. 8–9.

3. DECREE ON PEACE, ISSUED BY THE SECOND ALL-RUSSIA CONGRESS OF SOVIETS[3]

November 8 (October 26), 1917

The Workers' and Peasants' government, created by the revolution of October 24–25 and basing itself on the Soviets of Workers', Soldiers' and Peasants' Deputies, calls upon all the belligerent peoples and their governments to start immediate negotiations for a just, democratic peace.

By a just or democratic peace, for which the overwhelming majority of the working class and other working people of all the belligerent countries, exhausted, tormented and racked by the war, are craving—a peace that has been most definitely and insistently demanded by the Russian workers and peasants ever since the overthrow of the Tsarist monarchy—by such a peace the government means an immediate peace without annexations (i.e. without the seizure of foreign lands, without the forcible incorporation of foreign nations) and without indemnities.

The Government of Russia proposes that this kind of peace be immediately concluded by all the belligerent nations, and expresses its readiness to take all resolute measures now, without the least delay, pending the final ratification of all the terms of such a peace by authoritative assemblies of the people's representatives of all countries and all nations.

In accordance with the sense of justice of democrats in general, and of the working classes in particular, the Government conceives the annexation or seizure of foreign lands to mean every incorporation of a small or weak nation into a large or powerful state without the precisely, clearly and voluntarily expressed consent and wish of that nation, irrespective of the time when such forcible incorporation took place, irrespective also of the degree of development or backwardness of the nation forcibly annexed to the given state, or forcibly retained within its borders, and irrespective, finally, of whether this nation is in Europe or in distant, overseas countries.

If any nation whatsoever is forcibly retained within the borders of a given state, if, in spite of its expressed desire—no matter whether expressed in the press, at public meetings, in the decisions of parties, or in protests and uprising against national oppression—it is not accorded the right to decide the forms of its state existence by a free vote, taken after the complete evacuation of the troops of the incorporating or, generally, of the stronger nation and without the least pressure being brought to bear, such incorporation is annexation, i.e. seizure and violence.

The Government considers it the greatest of crimes against humanity to continue this war over the issue of how to divide among the strong and rich nations the weak nationalities they have conquered, and solemnly announces its determination immediately to sign terms of peace to stop this war on the terms indicated, which are equally just for all nationalities without exception.

At the same time the Government declares that it does not regard the above-mentioned peace terms as an ultimatum; in other words, it is prepared to consider any other peace terms, and insists only that they be advanced by any of the belligerent countries as speedily as possible, and that in the peace proposals there should be absolute clarity and the complete absence of all ambiguity and secrecy.

The Government abolishes secret diplomacy, and, for its part, announces its firm intention to conduct all negotiations quite openly in full view of the whole people. It will proceed immediately with the full publication of the secret treaties endorsed or concluded by the government of landowners and capitalists from February to October 25, 1917. The Government proclaims the unconditional and immediate annulment of everything contained in these secret treaties in so far as it is aimed, as is mostly the case, at securing advantages and privileges for the Russian landowners and capitalists and at the retention, or extension, of the annexations made by the Great Russians.

Proposing to the governments and peoples of all countries immediately to begin open negotiations for peace, the Government, for its part, expresses its readiness to conduct these negotiations in writing, by telegraph, and by negotiations between representatives of the various countries, or at a conference of such representatives. In order to facilitate such negotiations, the Government is appointing its plenipotentiary representative to neutral countries.

The Government proposes an immediate armistice to the governments and peoples of all the belligerent countries, and, for its part, considers it desirable that this armistice should be concluded for a period of not less than three months, i.e. a period long enough to permit the completion of negotiations for peace with the participation of the representatives of all peoples or nations, without exception, involved in or compelled to take part in the war, and the summoning of authoritative assemblies of the representatives of the peoples of all countries for the final ratification of the peace terms.

While addressing this proposal for peace to the governments and peoples of all the belligerent countries, the Provisional Workers' and Peasants' Government of Russia appeals in particular also to the class-conscious workers of the three most advanced nations of mankind and the largest states participating in the present war, namely, Great Britain, France and Germany. The workers of these countries have made the greatest contributions to the cause of progress and socialism; they have furnished the great examples of the Chartist movement in England, a number of revolutions of historic importance effected by the French proletariat, and, finally, the heroic struggle against the Anti-Socialist Law in Germany and the prolonged, persistent and disciplined work of creating mass proletarian organizations in Germany, a work which serves as a model to the workers of the whole world. All these examples of proletarian heroism and historical creative work are a pledge that the workers of the countries mentioned will understand the duty that now faces them of saving mankind from the horrors of war and its consequences, that these workers, by comprehensive, determined, and supremely vigorous action, will help us to conclude peace successfully, and at the same time emancipate the labouring and exploited masses of our population from all forms of slavery and all forms of exploitation.

Chairman of the Council of People's Commissars, VLADIMIR ULYANOV-LENIN

Decrees, Vol. 1, pp. 12–16.

4. DECREE ON LAND, ISSUED BY THE SECOND ALL-RUSSIA CONGRESS OF SOVIETS[4]

November 8 (October 26), 1917

(1) Landed proprietorship is abolished forthwith without any compensation.

(2) The landed estates, as also all crown, monastery, and church lands, with all their livestock, implements, buildings and everything pertaining thereto, shall be placed at the disposal of the *volost** land committees and the *uyezd*† Soviets of Peasants' Deputies pending the convocation of the Constituent Assembly.

(3) All damage to confiscated property, which henceforth belongs to the whole people, is proclaimed a grave crime to be punished by the revolutionary courts. The *uyezd* Soviets of Peasants' Deputies shall take all necessary measures to assure the observance of the strictest order during the confiscation of the landed estates, to determine the size of estates, and the particular estates subject to confiscation, to draw up exact inventories of all property confiscated and to protect in the strictest revolutionary way all agricultural enterprises transferred to the people, with all buildings, implements, livestock, stocks of produce, etc.

(4) The following peasant Mandate, complied by the newspaper *Izvestia Vserossiiskogo Soveta Krestyanskikh Deputatov* from 242 local peasant mandates and published in No. 88 of that paper (Petrograd, No. 88, August 19, 1917), shall serve everywhere to guide the implementation of the great land reforms until a final decision on the latter is taken by the Constituent Assembly.

ON LAND

"The land question in its full scope can be settled only by the popular Constituent Assembly.

"The most equitable settlement of the land question is to be as follows:

* The Russian "volost" was the lowest administrative unit of territory above the village.

† The "uyezd" was the next highest—Thus they correspond to "rural district" and "county" respectively (though much larger than the British units).

"(1) Private ownership of land shall be abolished for ever; land shall not be sold, purchased, leased, mortgaged, or otherwise alienated.

"All land, whether State, crown, monastery, church, factory, entailed, private, public, peasant, etc., shall be confiscated without compensation and become property of the whole people, and pass into the use of all those who cultivate it.

"Persons who suffer by this property revolution shall be deemed to be entitled to public support only for the period necessary for adaptation to the new conditions of life.

"(2) All mineral wealth—ore, oil, coal, salt, etc. and also all forests and waters of state importance, shall pass into the exclusive use of the State. All the small streams, lakes, woods, etc., shall pass into the use of the communes, to be administered by the local self-government bodies.

"(3) Lands on which high-level scientific farming is practised—orchards, plantations, seed plots, nurseries, hot-houses, etc.—shall not be divided up, but shall be converted into model farms, to be turned over for exclusive use to the state or to the communes, depending on the size and importance of such lands.

"Household land in towns and villages, with orchards and vegetable gardens, shall be reserved for the use of their present owners, the size of the holdings, and the size of tax levied for the use thereof, to be determined by law.

"(4) Stud farms, government and private pedigree stock and poultry farms, etc., shall be confiscated and become the property of the whole people, and pass into the exclusive use of the State or a commune, depending on the size and importance of such farms.

"The question of compensation shall be examined by the Constituent Assembly.

"(5) All livestock and farm implements of the confiscated estates shall pass into the exclusive use of the State or a commune, depending on their size and importance, and no compensation shall be paid for this.

"The farm implements of peasants with little land shall not be subject to confiscation.

"(6) The right to use the land shall be accorded to all

citizens of the Russian State (without distinction of sex) desiring to cultivate it by their own labour, with the help of their families, or in partnership, but only as long as they are able to cultivate it. The employment of hired labour is not permitted.

"In the event of the temporary physical disability of any member of a village commune for a period of up to two years, the village commune shall be obliged to assist him for this period by collectively cultivating his land until he is again able to work.

"Peasants who, owing to old age or ill health, are permanently disabled and unable to cultivate the land personally, shall lose their right to the use of it but, in return, shall receive a pension from the State.

"(7) Land tenure shall be on an equality basis, i.e. the land shall be distributed among the working people in conformity with a labour standard or a subsistence standard, depending on local conditions.

"There shall be absolutely no restriction on the forms of land tenure—household, farm, communal, or co-operative, as shall be decided in each individual village and settlement.

"(8) All land, when alienated, shall become part of the national land fund. Its distribution among the peasants shall be in charge of the local and central self-government bodies, from democratically organized village and city communes, in which there are no distinctions of social rank, to central regional government bodies.

"The land fund shall be subject to periodical redistribution, depending on the growth of population and the increase in the productivity and the scientific level of farming.

"When the boundaries of allotments are altered, the original nucleus of the allotment shall be left intact.

"The land of the members who leave the commune shall revert to the land fund; preferential right to such land shall be given to the near relatives of the members who have left, or to persons designated by the latter.

"The cost of fertilizers and improvements put into the land, to the extent that they have not been fully used up to the time the allotment is returned to the land fund, shall be compensated.

"Should the available land fund in a particular district prove inadequate for the needs of the local population, the surplus population shall be settled elsewhere.

"The State shall take upon itself the organization of resettlement and shall bear the cost thereof, as well as the cost of supplying implements, etc.

"Resettlement shall be effected in the following order: landless peasants desiring to resettle, then members of the commune who are of vicious habits, deserters, and so on, and, finally, by lot or by agreement."

The entire contents of this mandate, as expressing the absolute will of the vast majority of the class-conscious peasants of all Russia, is proclaimed a provisional law, which, pending the convocation of the Constituent Assembly, shall be carried into effect as far as possible immediately, and as to certain of its provisions with due gradualness, as shall be determined by the *uyezd* Soviets of Peasants' Deputies.

(5) The land of ordinary peasants and ordinary Cossacks shall not be confiscated.

Chairman of the Council of People's Commissars, VLADIMIR ULYANOV-LENIN.

October 26, 1917.

Decrees, Vol. 1, pp. 17–20.

5. DECREE OF THE SECOND ALL-RUSSIA CONGRESS OF SOVIETS TO FORM THE WORKERS' AND PEASANTS' GOVERNMENT[5]

November 8 (October 26), 1917

The All-Russia Congress of Soviets of Workers', Soldiers' and Peasants' Deputies resolves:

To establish a Provisional Workers' and Peasants' Government, to be known as the Council of People's Commissars, to govern the country until the Constituent Assembly is convened. The management of individual branches of state activity is entrusted to commissions whose members shall ensure the fulfilment of the programme announced by the Congress, and shall work in close contact with mass organizations of men and women workers, sailors, soldiers, peasants and office employees. Governmental authority is vested in a collegium of the chairmen of those commissions, i.e. the Council of People's Commissars.

Control over the activities of the People's Commissars with the right to replace them is vested in the All-Russia Congress of Soviets of Workers', Peasants' and Soldiers' Deputies and its Central Executive Committee.

At the present time the Council of People's Commissars is constituted as follows:

Chairman of the Council—Vladimir Ulyanov (Lenin);
People's Commissar of the Interior—A. I. Rykov;
Agriculture—V. P. Milyutin;
Labour—A. G. Shlyapnikov;
Army and Navy Affairs—a committee consisting of
V. A. Ovseyenko (Antonov), N. V. Krylenko and P. Y. Dybenko;
Commerce and Industry—V. P. Nogin;
Education—A. V. Lunacharsky;
Finance—I. Skvortsov (Stepanov);
Foreign Affairs—L. D. Bronstein (Trotsky);
Justice—G. I. Oppokov (Lomov);
Food—I. A. Teodorovich;

Post and Telegraph—N. P. Avilov (Glebov).
Chairman for Nationalities Affairs—J. V. Jugashvili (Stalin).
The office of the People's Commissar of Railways is temporarily vacant.

Decrees, Vol. 1, pp. 20–21.

6. DECREE ON THE PRESS, ISSUED BY THE COUNCIL OF PEOPLE'S COMMISSARS[6]

November 9 (October), 1917

In the trying critical period of the revolution and the days that immediately followed it the Provisional Revolutionary Committee was compelled to take a number of measures against the counter-revolutionary press of different shades.

Immediately outcries were heard from all sides that the new, socialist power had violated a fundamental principle of its programme by encroaching upon the freedom of the press.

The Workers' and Peasants' Government calls the attention of the population to the fact that what this liberal façade actually conceals is freedom for the propertied classes, having taken hold of the lion's share of the entire press, to poison, unhindered, the minds and obscure the consciousness of the masses.

Every one knows that the bourgeois press is one of the most powerful weapons of the bourgeoisie. Especially at the crucial moment when the new power, the power of workers and peasants, is only affirming itself, it was impossible to leave this weapon wholly in the hands of the enemy, for in such moments it is no less dangerous than bombs and machine-guns. That is why temporary extraordinary measures were taken to stem the torrent of filth and slander in which the yellow and green press would be only too glad to drown the recent victory of the people.

As soon as the new order becomes consolidated, all administrative pressure on the press will be terminated and it will be granted complete freedom within the bounds of legal responsibility, in keeping with a law that will be broadest and most progressive in this respect.

However, being aware that a restriction of the press, even at critical moments, is permissible only within the limits of what is absolutely necessary, the Council of People's Commissars resolves:

GENERAL PROVISIONS on the PRESS

1. Only those publications can be suppressed which (1) call

for open resistance or insubordination to the Workers' and Peasants' Government; (2) sow sedition through demonstrably slanderous distortion of facts; (3) instigate actions of an obviously criminal, i.e. criminally punishable, nature.

2. Publications can be proscribed, temporarily or permanently, only by decision of the Council of People's Commissars.

3. The present ordinance is of a temporary nature and will be repealed by a special decree as soon as normal conditions of social life set in.

Chairman of the Council of People's Commissars, VLADIMIR ULYANOV (LENIN).

Petrograd, October 27, 1917.

Decrees, Vol. 1, pp. 24–25.

7. DECLARATION OF RIGHTS OF THE PEOPLES OF RUSSIA

November 15 (2), 1917

The October Revolution of workers and peasants began under the common banner of emancipation.

The peasants are emancipated from landowner rule, for there is no landed proprietorship any longer—it has been abolished. The soldiers and sailors are emancipated from the power of autocratic generals, for generals will henceforth be elected and removable. The workers are emancipated from the whims and tyranny of capitalists, for workers' control over factories and mills will henceforth be established. All that is living and viable is emancipated from the hated bondage.

There remain only the peoples of Russia, who have been and are suffering from oppression and arbitrary rule, whose emancipation should be started immediately, and whose liberation should be conducted resolutely and irrevocably.

In the epoch of tsarism the peoples of Russia were systematically incited against one another. The results of this policy are known: massacres and pogroms, on the one side, and slavery of the peoples, on the other.

There is no return to this infamous policy of incitement. From now on it is to be replaced by a policy of voluntary and sincere alliance of the peoples of Russia.

In the period of imperialism, after the February Revolution, which had given power to the Constitutional-Democrat bourgeoisie, the undisguised policy of incitement ceded place to the policy of cowardly distrust towards the peoples of Russia, the policy of petty excuses for persecution and provocation covered up with utterances about "freedom" and "equality" of the peoples. The results of this policy are known: increased national enmity, undermined mutual confidence.

This reprehensible policy of lie and distrust, petty persecution and provocation must be done away with. From now on it shall be replaced by an open and honest policy leading to the complete mutual confidence of the peoples of Russia.

Only this confidence can lead to a sincere and firm alliance of the peoples of Russia.

Only thanks to this alliance can the workers and peasants of the peoples of Russia be welded into a single revolutionary force capable of holding out against any encroachments on the part of the imperialist-annexationist bourgeoisie.

Proceeding from these premises, the First Congress of Soviets in June of this year proclaimed the right of the peoples of Russia to free self-determination.

In October of this year the Second Congress of Soviets reaffirmed this inalienable right of the peoples of Russia more resolutely and definitely.

Carrying out the will of these Congresses, the Council of People's Commissars has resolved to base on its activity in the matter of the nationalities of Russia on the following principles:

1. Equality and sovereignty of the peoples of Russia.
2. The right of the peoples of Russia to free self-determination, up to secession and formation of an independent State.
3. Abolition of all and any national and national-religious privileges and restrictions.
4. Free development of national minorities and ethnic groups inhabiting Russia.

Concrete decrees stemming herefrom will be worked out immediately after the establishment of the Commission for the Affairs of Nationalities.

In the name of the Russian Republic,

People's Commissar for Nationalities Affairs,
JOSEPH JUGASHVILI-STALIN.
Chairman of the Council of People's Commissars, V. ULYANOV (LENIN).

November 2, 1917.

Decrees, Vol. 1, pp. 39–41.

8. DECREE ON THE REDUCTION OF THE ARMY ISSUED BY THE COUNCIL OF PEOPLE'S COMMISSARS[7]

November 23 (10), 1917

The Workers' and Peasants' Government of People's Commissars has resolved:

To start gradual reduction of the numerical strength of the army and, pursuant to this, to transfer forthwith to the indefinite reserve soldiers drafted in 1899. The ordinance regarding the draftees of other years will be issued later on. The dischargees shall hand over their weapons to the regimental committees which are responsible for their safekeeping.

The Supreme Commander-in-Chief shall announce this forthwith in an army order of the day.

Chairman of the Council of the People's Commissars, VL. ULYANOV (LENIN).
People's Commissars of Military Affairs, V. A. OVSEYENKO (ANTONOV), N. KRYLENKO.

Decrees, Vol. 1, p. 66.

9. DECREE ON THE ABOLITION OF SOCIAL ESTATES AND CIVIL RANKS, ISSUED BY THE ALL-RUSSIA CENTRAL EXECUTIVE COMMITTEE AND THE COUNCIL OF PEOPLE'S COMMISSARS [8]

November 24 (11), 1917

1. All the social estates and civil gradations, the privileges and restrictions stemming therefrom, the organizations and institutions of the estates, as well as all the civil ranks that have hitherto existed in Russia, are hereby abolished.

2. All designations of social standing (nobleman, merchant, petty bourgeois, peasant, etc.), title (prince, count, etc.) and civil rank (privy councillor, councillor of state, etc.) are abolished and a single designation of citizens of the Russian Republic is established for the entire population of Russia.

3. The property of noblemen's institutions is handed over forthwith to the respective district self-government bodies.

4. The property of merchant and petty bourgeois societies is placed forthwith at the disposal of the respective municipal authorities.

5. All the institutions of the social estates, their files, cases at bar and archives are placed forthwith under the jurisdiction of the respective municipal and district authorities.

6. All the relevant clauses of the heretofore effective laws are annulled.

7. The present Decree enters into force from the day of publication and is immediately enacted by the local Soviets of Workers', Soldiers' and Peasants' Deputies.

The present Decree was approved by the Central Executive Committee of the Soviets of Workers' and Soldiers' Deputies at a sitting on November 10, 1917.

Chairman of the Central Executive Committee, YA. SVERDLOV.
Chairman of the Council of People's Commissars, VL. ULYANOV (LENIN).

Business Manager of the Council of People's
Commissars, V. BONCH-BRUYEVICH.
Secretary of the Council, N. GORBUNOV.

November 11, 1917.

Decrees, Vol. 1, p. 72.

10. INSTRUCTIONS OF THE ALL-RUSSIA CENTRAL EXECUTIVE COMMITTEE AND THE COUNCIL OF PEOPLE'S COMMISSARS ON WORKERS' CONTROL[9]

November 27 (14), 1917

1. In order to provide planned regulation of the national economy, workers' control over the manufacture, purchase, sale and storage of produce and raw materials and over the financial activity of enterprise is introduced in all industrial, commercial, banking, agricultural, cooperative and other enterprises which employ hired labour or give work to be done at home.

2. Workers' control is exercised by all the workers of the given enterprise through their elected bodies, such as factory committees, shop stewards' councils, etc., whose members include representatives of the office employees and the technical personnel.

3. In every city, *gubernia** and industrial district a local workers' control council is set up which, being an agency of the Soviet of Workers', Soldiers' and Peasants' Deputies, is composed of representatives of trade unions, factory and office workers' committees, and workers' cooperatives.

4. Pending the convocation of the congress of workers' control councils, an All-Russia Workers' Control Council is instituted in Petrograd, with the following representation: five members from the All-Russia Central Executive Committee of the Soviet of Workers' and Soldiers' Deputies; five from the All-Russia Central Executive Committee of Peasants Deputies; five from the All-Russia Council of Trade Unions; two from the All-Russia Workers' Cooperative Centre; five from the All-Russia Bureau of Factory Committees; five from the All-Russia Union of Engineers and Technicians; two from the All-Russia Union of Agronomists; one from every all-Russia union of workers having less than 100,000 members; two from

*"Gubernia" (sometimes translated wrongly as "government") was the next highest territorial unit in Tsarist Russia above the *uyezd*. It would be best rendered as "province".

every all-Russia union of workers having more than 100,000 members; two from the Petrograd Council of Trade Unions.

5. The supreme bodies of workers' control establish inspection commissions of specialists (technicians, bookkeepers, etc.) which are dispatched, either on the initiative of these bodies or at the insistance of lower workers' control bodies, to inspect the financial and technical activities of an enterprise.

6. The workers' control bodies have the right to supervise production, establish output quotas and take measures to ascertain production costs.

7. The workers' control bodies have the right of access to the entire business correspondence of an enterprise, concealment of the same by the owners is punishable by a court of law. Commercial secrecy is abolished. The owners are obliged to present to workers' control bodies all books and accounts for both the current and previous fiscal years.

8. Decisions of workers' control bodies are binding upon the owners of enterprises and may be revoked only by higher workers' control bodies.

9. The entrepreneur or the enterprise management has three days within which to appeal to a higher workers' control body against decisions of lower bodies of workers' control.

10. At all enterprises the owners and the representatives of the wage and salary earners elected to exercise workers' control are declared answerable to the state for the maintenance of the strictest order and discipline and for the protection of property. Those guilty of concealment of materials, products and orders, improper keeping of accounts and other such malpractices are held criminally responsible.

11. The district (as in Paragraph 3) workers' control councils settle all disputes and conflicts between lower control bodies, handle owners' complaints, issue instructions conformably with the specificity of production, the local conditions and the decisions and instructions of the All-Russia Workers' Control Council, and supervise the activity of the lower control bodies.

12. The All-Russia Workers' Control Council works out general plans of workers' control, issues instructions and ordinances, regulates relationships between district workers' control councils, and serves as the highest instance for all matters pertaining to workers' control.

13. The All-Russia Workers' Control Council coordinates the activity of workers' control bodies with that of all other institutions concerned with the organization of the national economy.

Instructions on the relationships between the All-Russia Workers' Control Council and other institutions organizing and regulating the national economy will be issued separately.

14. All laws and circulars hampering the activity of the factory and other committees and councils of wage and salary earners are repealed.

In the name of the Government of the Russian Republic,

Chairman of the Council of People's Commissars, VL. ULYANOV (LENIN).

People's Commissar of Labour, ALEXANDER SHLYAPNIKOV.

Business Manager of the Council of People's Commissars, VL. BONCH-BRUYEVICH.

Secretary of the Council, N. GORBUNOV.

Decrees, Vol. 1, pp. 83–85.

11. APPEAL OF THE COUNCIL OF PEOPLE'S COMMISSARS TO THE PEOPLES OF THE BELLIGERENT COUNTRIES

Not later than November 27 (14), 1917

In reply to our proposal of an immediate armistice on all fronts with a view to concluding a democratic peace—without annexations or indemnities, and respecting the right of nations to self-determination—the German commander-in-chief has expressed consent to holding peace talks. The supreme commander-in-chief of the Republic, Ensign Krylenko, has suggested postponing the commencement of the talks by five days, i.e. till November 19 (December 1*), in order to renew the proposal to the Allied governments to determine their attitude towards peace talks. By mutual agreement, hostilities on the Russian front have been suspended. It stands to reason that there should be no troop movements on either side within these five days.

A decisive step has been made. The victorious workers' and peasants' revolution in Russia has put the question of peace point-blank. The period of vacillations, procrastinations and bureaucratic agreements is over. Today all governments, all classes, all parties of the belligerent powers are required to answer unequivocably whether they agree to start together with us, on November 19 (December 1), negotiations on an immediate armistice and universal peace. Yes or No? It depends on their reply to this question whether the toilers of factory and field will be spared a new winter campaign with all its horrors and disasters, or Europe will go on bleeding.

We the Council of People's Commissars address this question to the governments of our allies: France, Great Britain, Italy, the United States, Belgium, Serbia, Rumania, Japan, China. We ask them before their own peoples, before the whole world whether they are prepared to commence, together with us, peace talks on December 1.

We the Council of People's Commissars ask the allied peoples and above all their toiling masses: whether they wish to drag on this slaughter without sense or aim, blindly proceed-

* Here and hereafter a mistake, to read December 2.

ing towards the doom of all European culture. We demand that the workers' parties of the allied countries immediately answer whether they want peace talks to open on December 1.

The question has been put point-blank. Soldiers, proletarians, working people, peasants, do you want to make together with us a resolute step toward peace for the peoples?

We the Council of People's Commissars appeal to the toiling masses of Germany, Austria-Hungary, Turkey, Bulgaria. The peace we have offered should be a peace for the peoples. It should be an honest agreement securing for every people the freedom of economic and cultural development. Such a peace can be concluded only through honest and courageous struggle of the revolutionary masses against all imperialist plans and aggressive aspirations.

The workers' and peasants' revolution has already set forth its peace programme. We have published the secret treaties of the tsar and the bourgeoisie with the allies and have declared these treaties not binding on the Russian people. We propose to all peoples a new treaty openly concluded on the principles of concord and cooperation.

In reply to our proposal official and semi-official circles of the ruling classes in the allied countries have refused to extend recognition to the Government of the Soviets and to reach accord with it on peace talks. The government of the victorious revolution stands in no need of recognition by the professionals of capitalist diplomacy. But we ask the peoples whether reactionary diplomacy expresses their thoughts and aspirations. Will the peoples let diplomacy miss the great opportunity of peace offered by the Russian revolution? The reply to these questions must be given immediately, and not in words but in deeds. The Russian army and the Russian people cannot, and do not want to, wait any longer. On December 1 we begin peace talks. If the allied nations do not dispatch their representatives, we will negotiate with the Germans single-handed. We want universal peace. But if the bourgeoisie of the allied countries compels us to conclude a separate peace, all the responsibility for this will fall on it.

Soldiers, workers and peasants of France, Britain, Italy, the United States, Belgium, Serbia! Peace talks are opening on December 1. We are awaiting your representatives. Act! Do not waste a single hour! Down with the winter campaign, down with the war!

Long live peace and the fraternity of nations!

Commissar for Foreign Affairs, L. TROTSKY.
Chairman of the Council of People's Commissars, V. ULYANOV (N. LENIN).

Decrees, Vol. I, pp. 86–88.

12. DECREE ON THE RIGHT OF RECALL, ISSUED BY THE ALL-RUSSIA CENTRAL EXECUTIVE COMMITTEE[10]

December 4 (November 21), 1917

No elective institution or representative assembly can be regarded as being truly democratic and really representative of the people's will unless the electors' right to recall those elected is accepted and exercised. This fundamental principle of true democracy applies to all representative assemblies without exception, including the Constituent Assembly.

Because the system of proportional representation is more democratic than the majority system, it demands more complex measures for the exercise of the right of recall, that is, the actual subordination of the elected to the people. But it would be betraying democracy and abdicating the basic principles and tasks of the socialist revolution, which has begun in Russia, to refuse, on that ground, to practise the right of recall, or to hamper or restrict its exercise in any way. What proportional representation demands is not abolition of the right of recall but a mere change of form.

Since the system of proportional representation is based on acceptance of the party system and the conduct of elections by organized parties, any major change in the balance of class forces and the relation of classes to parties, necessarily produces the need for a re-election in any electoral district where there is a clear and obvious discrepancy between the will of the various classes and their strength, on the one hand, and the party composition of those elected, on the other. True democracy makes it imperative that the appointment of re-elections should not depend only on the institution to be re-elected, that is, that the desire on the part of those elected to retain their seats should not work against the exercise of the people's will to recall its representatives.

In view of this, the All-Russia Central Executive Committee of the Soviets of Workers', Soldiers' and Peasants' Deputies, resolves:

The congress of the Soviets of Workers' and Soldiers' Deputies and the Soviets of Peasants' Deputies convened on a parity basis in each electoral district shall have the right to appoint re-elections to all city, *zemstvo* and all other representative institutions in general, not excluding the Constituent Assembly.

The Soviets shall order re-elections if so demanded by more than half of the electorate of the given electoral district.

The re-elections shall be held in the usual manner in strict conformity with the principles of proportional representation.

The newly-elected representatives shall, from the moment of election, supersede those recalled.

Decrees, Vol. 2, pp. 116–119.

13. DECREE ON THE JUDICATURE, ISSUED BY THE COUNCIL OF PEOPLE'S COMMISSARS[11]

December 5 (November 22), 1917.

The Council of People's Commissars resolves:

(1) To abolish the existing general judicial institutions, such as district courts, court chambers and the Senate Directing with all its departments, the military and naval courts of all designations, and commercial courts, replacing these by courts established through democratic elections.

A special decree will be issued on the order of continuation of pending cases.

All terms shall be suspended from October 25 of this year, until the issue of a special decree.

(2) To suspend the operation of the existing institution of justices of the peace, replacing justices of the peace, hitherto elected indirectly, by local courts as represented by a permanent local judge and two alternate assessors invited to every session in accordance with special lists. Local judges shall henceforth be elected on the basis of direct democratic suffrage; pending such elections they shall be elected by district and *volost* Soviets of Workers', Soldiers' and Peasants' Deputies or, in the absence of such, by *uyezd*, city and *gubernia* Soviets.

The same Soviets draw up lists of alternate assessors and determine the order of their attendance at sessions.

The former justices of the peace are not deprived of the right to be elected—should they so desire—local judges, both provisionally by the Soviets and definitively in democratic elections.

The local courts try all civil cases involving sums of not more than 3,000 roubles, and criminal cases punishable with not more than two years of prison and involving a civil suit not exceeding 3,000 roubles. Judgements passed by the local courts are final and without appeal. In cases where a recovery of more than 100 roubles or a prison term of more than seven days has been adjudged, a cassation request is allowed, with the *uyezd* court or, in the capitals, the metropolitan congress of local judges, serving as the cassation instance.

In the army in the field criminal cases are tried by local courts elected in the same manner by regimental councils or, in the absence of such, by regimental committees.

A special decree will be issued on court procedure to be followed in other cases.

(3) To abolish the existing institutions of court investigators, the procurator's surveillance, and official and private counsellors at law.

Pending the reorganization of the entire court procedure, preliminary criminal investigation shall be conducted personally by local judges, whose warrants for apprehension and bringing to trial shall be subject to approval by a full local court.

The functions of prosecution and defence, also in the preliminary investigation stage, and those of attorneys in civil cases, can be performed by all citizens, without distinction of sex, who are of good character and enjoy civil rights.

(4) Current cases and proceedings of judicial institutions, and those before officers of preliminary investigation, the procurator's surveillance and councils of the bar, as well as the archives and property of these institutions, are taken over by special commissars elected by the local Soviets of Workers', Soldiers' and Peasants' Deputies.

The junior and clerical personnel of the abolished institutions shall be obliged to continue in office, performing under the general direction of the commissars, all the necessary work on the referral of pendent cases and informing on fixed days, persons concerned about the progress of their cases.

(5) The local courts adjudicate in the name of the Russian Republic and abide by the laws of the overthrown governments insofar as such laws have not been abrogated by the revolution and do not contradict revolutionary conscience and revolutionary legal awareness.

NOTE. All laws contravening the decrees of the Central Executive Committee of the Soviets' of Workers, Soldiers' and Peasants' Deputies and also the minimum programmes of the Russian Social-Democratic Labour Party and the Socialist-Revolutionary Party shall be considered invalid.

(6) The sides involved in disputes over civil and private criminal matters may apply to the arbitration court. The order of arbitration will be determined by a special decree.

(7) The right of pardon and reinstatement in rights of convicted criminal offenders will rest henceforth with the judicial authority.

(8) In order to fight the counter-revolutionary forces and to protect the revolution and its gains against them, and also for the purpose of trying cases of marauding and pillage and the sabotage and other misdeeds of merchants, industrialists, officials and other persons, worker-and-peasant revolutionary tribunals shall be instituted consisting of a chairman and six alternate assessors elected by the *gubernia* or city Soviets of Workers', Soldiers' and Peasants' Deputies.

Special investigation commissions shall be instituted by the same Soviets to conduct preliminary inquiry into such cases.

All the hitherto existing investigation commissions are abolished and their cases and proceedings are turned over to the new investigation commissions to be set up by the Soviets.

Chairman of the Council of People's Commissars, V. ULYANOV (LENIN).
Commissars: A. SHLIKHTER, A. SHLYAPNIKOV, J. JUGASHVILI (STALIN), N. AVILOV (N. GLEBOV). P. STUCHKA.

Decrees, Vol. 1, pp. 124–126.

14. DECISION OF THE COUNCIL OF PEOPLE'S COMMISSARS ON THE RIGHTS OF LOCAL SOVIETS IN COMBATING SABOTAGE BY EMPLOYERS AND ON THE RULES OF CONFISCATING SABOTEURS' ENTERPRISES

December 7 (November 24), 1917

Regarding the enquiries coming in from local Soviets about measures to combat employers' sabotage, the Council of People's Commissars explains: (1) Local Soviets are entitled to take all measures against such employers, including confiscation of their enterprises; (2) Management of the confiscated enterprises is turned over to appropriate production regulation bodies; (3) In every instance the confiscation of an enterprise shall be preceded by an investigation into the state of affairs at the enterprise, especially as regards finance, fuel and raw material supply, and technical equipment; (4) In the case of joint-stock companies confiscation extends to all the cash capital belonging to them; in the case of enterprise belonging to partnerships or individuals, confiscation extends to the cash capital of the shareholders and the individual owners, inasmuch as these persons are held answerable with all their property should the enterprise prove insolvent; (5) All funds of confiscated enterprises, including those of current accounts in private banks, shall be deposited in the State Bank.

Chairman of the Council of People's Commissars, V. ULYANOV (LENIN).
People's Commissars:
Business Manager of the Council of People's Commissars, V. BONCH-BRUYEVICH.
Secretary of the Council, N. GORBUNOV.

November 24, 1917.

Decrees, Vol. 1, p. 546.

15. DECREE OF THE COUNCIL OF PEOPLE'S COMMISSARS ON MONOPOLY STATE CONTROL OF FARM MACHINES AND IMPLEMENTS[12]

December 8 (November 25), 1917

In the name of the Republic the Council of People's Commissars resolves:

1. In order to provide agriculture with means of production and meet the needs of the working people of the countryside, all farm machines and implements manufactured at home or imported from other countries are hereby declared a monopoly possession of the state.

2. The distribution of such machines and implements shall be effected, in keeping with the rules to be issued separately, through bodies of Soviet power, land committees, and other democratic organizations.

Chairman of the Council of People's Commissars, V. ULYANOV (LENIN)

People's Commissar for Food Supplies, A. SHLIKHTER.

Commissar of the Department for the Supply of Implements of Production and Metals to Africulture, KOZMIN.

Business Manager of the Council, VL. BONCH-BRUYEVICH.

Secretary of the Council, N. GORBUNOV.

November 25, 1917.

Decrees, Vol. 1, p. 148.

16. DECREE OF THE COUNCIL OF PEOPLE'S COMMISSARS ON THE ARREST OF LEADERS OF THE CIVIL WAR AGAINST THE REVOLUTION[13]

December 11 (November 28), 1917

Members of the leading bodies of the Constitutional-Democratic Party, which is a party of enemies of the people, shall be arrested and brought before revolutionary tribunals.

Local Soviets are instructed to exercise special surveillance over the CDP in view of its association with the Kornilov-Kaledin civil war against the revolution.

This decree enters into effect from the time of signing.

Chairman of the Council of People's Commissars, VL. ULYANOV (LENIN).
People's Commissars: N. AVILOV (N. GLEBOV), P. STUCHKA, V. MENZHINSKY, JUGASHVILI-STALIN, G. PETROVSKY, A. SHLIKHTER, P. DYBENKO.
Business Manager of the Council of People's Commissars, VLAD. BONCH-BRUYEVICH.
Secretary of the Council, N. GORBUNOV.

Petrograd, November 28, 1917, 10.30 p.m.

Decrees, Vol. 1, p. 162.

17. DECREE OF THE ALL-RUSSIA CENTRAL EXECUTIVE COMMITTEE AND THE COUNCIL OF PEOPLE'S COMMISSARS ON THE ESTABLISHMENT OF THE SUPREME ECONOMIC COUNCIL[14]

December 15 (2), 1917

(1) A Supreme Economic Council is hereby established within the framework of the Council of People's Commissars.

(2) The task of the Supreme Economic Council is organization of the national economy and state finance. With this aim in view the Supreme Economic Council works out guidelines and plans for regulating the country's economy; coordinates and unifies the activity of central and local regulating institutions (conferences on fuel, metal, transport, the Central Food Committee, etc.), the corresponding people's commissariats (of trade and industry, food supplies, agriculture, finance, army and navy, etc.), the All-Russia Workers' Control Council, as well as the relevant activity of working-class organizations.

(3) The Supreme Economic Council is vested with the right of confiscation, requisitioning, sequestering and compulsory syndication of branches of industry and trade and of taking other measures in the field of production, distribution and state finance.

(4) All institutions concerned with regulation of the economy are subordinated to the Supreme Economic Council, which is authorized to reform them.

(5) The Supreme Economic Council is composed of: (*a*) the All Russia Workers' Control Council, as constituted by the decree of November 14, 1917; (*b*) representatives of all the People's Commissariats; (*c*) experts with a voice but no vote.

(6) The Supreme Economic Council is divided into sections and departments (fuel, metal, demobilization, finance, etc.), whose number and jurisdiction are determined by a general meeting of the Supreme Economic Council.

(7) The departments of the Supreme Economic Council are engaged in regulating separate areas of economic life and in preparing measures to be carried out by the respective People's Commissariats.

(8) The Supreme Economic Council appoints a bureau of 15 members to coordinate the day-to-day work of the sections and departments and deal with tasks requiring immediate solution.

(9) All draft laws and major projects pertaining to the regulation of the national economy as a whole are submitted to the Council of People's Commissars through the Supreme Economic Council.

(10) The Supreme Economic Council unifies and directs the work of the local economic departments of the Soviets of Workers', Soldiers' and Peasants' Deputies which incorporate local workers' control bodies, and the work of the local commissariats of labour, trade and industry, food supplies, etc.

Wherever such economic departments do not exist the Supreme Economic Council establishes its own local bodies.

All decisions of the Supreme Economic Council are binding on the economic departments of the local Soviets which are local bodies of the Supreme Economic Council.

Chairman of the Central Executive Committee, Y. SVERDLOV.
Chairman of the Council of People's Commissars, VL. ULYANOV (LENIN).
People's Commissars: J. STALIN, N. AVILOV (N. GLEBOV).
Business Manager of the Council of People's Commissars, VL. BONCH-BRUYEVICH.
Secretary, N. GLEBOV.

Decrees, Vol. 1, pp. 172–174.

18. APPEAL OF THE ALL-RUSSIA CENTRAL EXECUTIVE COMMITTEE AND OTHER ORGANIZATIONS TO THE TOILING MASSES OF ALL COUNTRIES

December 21 (8), 1917

The October armed uprising of the toiling masses of Russia removed from power the bourgeois imperialists and their servitors and installed a government in the shape of the Council of People's Commissars. This government of the workers, soldiers and peasants of Russia has proposed that all belligerent countries conclude an armistice on all fronts and enter upon negotiations on a universal democratic peace. Representatives of Russia and the Central Powers met on December 2. The delegation of Russian democracy deemed it its primary duty to stress to the representatives of the Central Powers that its objective was not a separate armistice and peace but universal peace on the principles proclaimed by the Russian revolution. With this aim in view the Russian delegates proposed to the Central Powers to address all the belligerent sovereign Powers not represented at the conference with a direct invitation to conclude an armistice. At the same time the Russian delegates laid down the condition that no troops of the Central Powers should be redeployed from the Russian to the Western front during the armistice. On December 5 the armistice was concluded. The terms of the Russian delegation were accepted. The joint meeting of workers, soldiers and peasants fully supports this policy of the Workers' and Peasants' Government, for it opens the way to universal peace.

The joint meeting appeals to you, workers of Germany. You, to whom the predatory aims of German imperialism are as alien as the aggressive aspirations of Russian imperialism are to us, should support in every way the struggle of the Russian people for a just universal peace. Are you fighting to die, not on the Vistula but on the Isère? In town and country, in the factories and in the trenches you should carry on the most active fight for peace and prevent the imperialists from wrecking the talks that have been started.

And let your rulers not tell you that only by a victorious continuation of the war can you force peace upon the governments of France and Britain. The imperialists of Britain, France and the United States are telling the same to their own peoples. It is for three years now that the peoples have been shedding blood on all fronts, but neither victories nor defeats have brought nearer the longed-for peace. Only the will of the peoples can compel the imperialists of all countries to conclude a democratic peace.

Workers of France, Britain and Italy, peoples of blood-soaked Serbia and ravaged Belgium! You too should raise your voice. Let your governments know that you are no longer willing to shed blood for annexionist aims alien to you. We representatives of the toiling masses of Russia cannot secure universal peace all by ourselves. You should demand that your representatives, too, take part in the talks.

But even that will not suffice. We do not want a peace that would sanctify the old injustices, forge new chains and burden the working people with the grievous consequences of the war. We want a peace of the peoples, a democratic peace, a just peace. But we shall secure such a peace only when the peoples of all countries dictate its terms by their revolutionary struggle—if not only Russia but all other countries send to the peace conference representatives of the popular masses and not those of capitalism and militarism.

On behalf of many millions of working people the joint meeting of workers', soldiers' and peasants' deputies calls upon you, workers of all lands, to fight for a general armistice, for universal peace without annexations and indemnities, based on self-determination of nations!

Long live the international revolutionary struggle of workers, soldiers and peasants!

Long live Socialism!

All-Russia Central Executive Committee of Workers', Soldiers' and Peasants' Deputies,
All-Russia Peasants' Congress, Petrograd Soviet of Workers' and Soldiers' Deputies,
Red Guard Headquarters,
Representatives of Trade Unions, factory

committees, regimental committees, and district Soviets of Workers' and Soldiers' Deputies

Decrees, Vol. 1, pp. 118–189.

19. RULES FOR UNEMPLOYMENT INSURANCE ADOPTED BY THE ALL-RUSSIA CENTRAL EXECUTIVE COMMITTEE AND THE COUNCIL OF PEOPLE'S COMMISSARS[15]

December 24 (11), 1917

(1) The present Rules are effective throughout the Russian Republic and apply to all gainfully employed persons irrespective of sex, age, occupation and of whether they work for a state, public or private establishment or for an individual.

(2) The present Rules do not apply to persons whose regular earnings exceed three-fold the average earnings of the workers in the given locality as estimated by the local or regional council of trade unions.

(3) The present Rules regard as unemployed any able-bodied person for whom work for hire is the principal source of subsistence and who is unable to find work for the rate of remuneration established by the trade unions or, in the absence of such, by the labour exchange and who has been registered by the local labour exchange or trade unions or, in the absence of such, by the local mutual aid societies.

NOTE. Persons unable to earn a living as a result of a lock-out are regarded as unemployed.

(4) The present Rules do not regard as unemployed: (*a*) persons who have lost their work without losing their earnings; (*b*) persons who have lost their earnings as a result of a strike—for the duration of the strike; (*c*) persons who, as established by the local unemployment insurance committee or agencies authorized by it, have quit work or failed to take up new work without valid reasons, or those not in need of unemployment relief at the present time.

(5) The fact of unemployment and how long a person has been out of work is established by the local unemployment insurance committee through the labour exchange and trade unions.

(6) The means out of which unemployment benefits are paid are made up of deductions from the progressive tax on incomes, property and inheritance.

(7) Pending the introduction of such tax these means are made up of dues paid by the employers.

(8) Such dues are paid to the local unemployment insurance fund and form an all-Russia unemployment insurance fund. The latter is administered according to the rules worked out by the Central Unemployment Insurance Commission (Clause 25).

(9) The size of the employers' dues to be paid to the unemployment insurance fund is fixed in percentage terms by the Central Unemployment Insurance Commission, according to the same principle throughout Russia, at not less than three per cent of the wages on the bases of the data supplied by the all-Russia Council of Trade Unions. In the case of season-workers the minimum is five per cent.

(10) By decision of the local unemployment insurance committee or the *gubernia* or Central Unemployment Insurance Commission dues can be paid according to grades instead of in percentages of the wages.

(11) The dues are paid to the local unemployment insurance fund within a week after the pay day. Arrears are exacted by decision of the commissar of labour as an incontestable collection by the state; in addition, the employers are required to pay to the unemployment insurance fund a monthly fine equalling ten per cent of the sum in arrear, with every short month regarded as a full one.

(12) In relation to the unemployment insurance committee the employers are required: (*a*) to report within a week's time about every new hired or dismissed worker; (*b*) to furnish information data in the order established by the Central Unemployment Insurance Commission, on the earnings of every employee; (*c*) to keep record of these data; (*d*) to produce documents, accounts, records and books confirming these data for inspection by authorized representatives of the unemployment insurance committee.

(13) The present Rules regard as earnings: (*a*) the sum earned within a specific period of time in the form of salary or wages (no matter whether issued on the piece-rate, daily, monthly or any other basis), including overtime pay; (*b*) remuneration in kind (lodging, board, etc.), if any, with the cost of lodging rated at 20 per cent of the earnings and the

cost of board, etc., at its actual value; (*c*) the employee's share in the profits and the bonus received by him.

(14) The unemployment benefit equals the average daily earnings in the given locality but cannot exceed the sum that was actually earned by the recipient. The moment from which benefits begin to be paid is determined, after the establishment of the local unemployment insurance fund, by the Central Unemployment Insurance Commission, which allocates the necessary means for it. Depending on circumstances, the Central Unemployment Insurance Commission may reduce the unemployment benefit rate established by the present clause.

NOTE. The average earnings in the given locality are determined by the local or regional council of trade unions.

(15) An unemployed person is entitled to a benefit beginning from the fourth day of unemployment.

(16) In case of an illness of an unemployed person who is not entitled to assistance from the mutual aid society, the local unemployment insurance committee enters upon an agreement with the latter on rendering him assistance during his illness according to the mutual aid society's rates, with the expenses to be defrayed by the local unemployment insurance fund.

(17) Local unemployment insurance funds are instituted forthwith in all cities and other inhabited localities having more than 20,000 residents. In other localities such funds are instituted for areas whose boundaries are established by the *gubernia* unemployment insurance commission and approved by the Central Unemployment Insurance Commission.

(18) The local unemployment insurance funds have the right to form unions and enter upon agreements both among themselves and with other organizations and institutions.

(19) The local unemployment insurance funds may acquire, in their name, proprietary rights, including the right to real estates, conclude contracts, and sue and be sued in a court of law.

(20) The affairs of the local unemployment insurance funds are managed by a committee three-quarters of which represent the local council of trade unions and one-quarter the local mutual aid society. If the given locality has neither a council of trade unions nor a single mutual aid society, the delegates of the local trade unions and mutual aid societies gather separately and elect their share of representatives.

(21) The unemployment insurance committee appoints from among its members a board and an auditing commission.

(22) Under the present Rules, decisions of the local unemployment insurance committee can be appealed against within a term of two weeks to the *gubernia* unemployment insurance commission, and those of the latter, within the same term, to the Central Commission (Clause 25). The lodging of an appeal does not suspend the execution of decisions.

(23) Under the present Rules, the functions of *gubernia* courts of arbitration on unemployment insurance matters and of *gubernia* unemployment insurance councils are performed by the *gubernia* and central unemployment insurance commissions.

(24) The *gubernia* unemployment insurance commission consists of 19 members, ten representing the council of trade unions; four, the mutual aid societies; one, the labour exchange; one, the Commissariat of Labour; one, the Commissariat of Trade and Industry; one, the city authority and one, the *zemstvo* authority.

(25) The Central Unemployment Insurance Commission, with the office in Petrograd, consists of 23 members, 13 representing the All-Russia Council of Trade Unions; five, the workers' unemployment insurance group attached to the Unemployment Insurance Council; two, the Commissariat of Labour; one, the Commissariat of Trade and Industry; one, the All-Russia Union of Zemstvos and one, the All-Russia Union of Cities.

NOTE. The Central Commission has the right to issue ordinances and instructions, which are binding on all local unemployment insurance committees and *gubernia* commissions.

(26) The councils of trade unions or, in the absence of such, assemblies of representatives of trade unions and mutual aid societies are required to direct the institution of unemployment insurance funds, *gubernia* commissions and the Central Commission.

(27) Should the organizations cited in Clause 26 fail to initiate, within one month, the establishment of unemployment insurance funds, the latter will be instituted by order of the Commissar of Labour.

(28) The present Rules come into force forthwith and are given effect by telegraph. Violation of the Rules involves punishment by a court of law of up to one year in prison.

Chairman of the Central Executive Committee, SVERDLOV.
Chairman of the Council of People's Commissars, VL. ULYANOV (LENIN).
People's Commissar of Labour, A. SHLYAPNIKOV.
Business Manager of the Council, VLAD. BONCH-BRUYEVICH.
Secretary of the Council, N. GORBUNOV.

December 11, 1917.

Decrees, Vol. 1, pp. 201–204.

20. DECISION OF THE COUNCIL OF PEOPLE'S COMMISSARS ON THE TRANSFERENCE OF MATTERS OF EDUCATION AND UPBRINGING FROM THE JURISDICTION OF CLERICAL AUTHORITIES TO THAT OF THE PEOPLE'S COMMISSARIAT OF PUBLIC EDUCATION[16]

December 24 (11), 1917

In view of the ambiguity of the decisions of the previous ministries regarding the transference of parish schools to the jurisdiction of the Ministry of Public Education, which is evidenced by numerous queries from the provinces, the Commissariat of Public Education (formerly the Ministry of Public Education) has re-examined the question and resolved: to transfer matters of education and upbringing from the jurisdiction of the clerical authorities to that of the Commissariat of Public Education. The transference concerns all parish (primary, one-year, two-year) schools, teachers' seminaries, ecclesiastical schools and seminaries, diocesan women's schools, missionary schools, academies and all other church-administered primary, secondary and higher schools and institutions of different designations, together with their staffs, allocated funds, movable and immovable property such as buildings, outbuildings and the land under them, the school plots of land, farms (if any), libraries and all kinds of instructional aids, valuables, capital and securities and interest on them, and everything that was allotted to the aforesaid schools and institutions.

The question of the churches at these establishments will be decided along with the enactment of a decree on the separation of church from state.

Chairman of the Council of People's Commissars, VL. ULYANOV (LENIN).
Secretary of the Council of People's Commissars, N. GORBUNOV.
People's Commissar, A. V. LUNACHARSKY.

Government Commissar of the Public Schools Department, VL. GALKIN.
Secretary, DM. LESHCHENKO.

December 11, 1917.

Decrees, Vol. 1, pp. 210–211.

21. DECREE ON NATIONALIZATION OF BANKS, ISSUED BY THE ALL-RUSSIA CENTRAL EXECUTIVE COMMITTEE[17]

December 27 (14), 1917

In the interest of correct organization of the national economy, in the interest of resolute eradication of banking speculation and complete emancipation of the workers, peasants and the entire working population from exploitation by bank capital, and with the aim of establishing a single people's bank of the Russian Republic truly to serve the people and the poorest classes, the Central Executive Committee resolves:

(1) Banking is hereby declared a monopoly of the state.

(2) All existing private joint-stock banks and banking houses are merged with the State Bank.

(3) The assets and liabilities of the liquidated enterprises are taken over by the State Bank.

(4) The order of merger of private banks with the State Bank is determined by a special decree.

(5) Management of the affairs of private banks is temporarily vested in the council of the State Bank.

(6) The interests of small depositors shall be fully guaranteed.

Decrees, Vol. 1, p. 230.

22. DECREE ON DIVORCE, ISSUED BY THE ALL-RUSSIA CENTRAL EXECUTIVE COMMITTEE AND THE COUNCIL OF PEOPLE'S COMMISSARS

December 29 (16), 1917

1. Marriage is dissolved at the request of both spouses or either of them.

2. Such request is addressed, in keeping with the rules of venue, to the local court.

NOTE. By mutual agreement, the divorce application can be handed in directly to the marriage registration department where the given marriage was registered, which department registers the dissolution of marriage and issues a certificate thereof.

3. On the day appointed for hearing the divorce application the local judge summons both spouses or their attorneys.

4. If the place of residence of the spouse due to be summoned is unknown, the divorce application can be handed in at the last place of residence of the absent spouse known to the applicant, or at the applicant's place of residence, with the indication of the last known address of the respondent.

5. If the address of the absent spouse is unknown, the hearing is held at earliest two months after the publication of the announcement of the summons in the local government newspaper, and the summons is sent to the last known address of the respondent indicated by the applicant.

6. Having satisfied himself that the dissolution of marriage is really requested by both spouses or one of them, the judge personally declares the marriage dissolved and issues a certificate thereof. The judge also forwards a copy of his ruling to the marriage registration department where the marriage was consummated and where the relevant register is kept.

7. In the event of divorce by mutual consent the spouses are bound to indicate in their application what family names they and their children will henceforth bear. In the event of divorce requested by one spouse and of the absence of agreement on this matter the divorcees retain their pre-marital names, while the family names of the children are decided upon by the judge, or, should a dispute arise, by the local court.

8. On mutual agreement between the spouses, the judge, along with declaring the marriage dissolved, decides which of the parents will keep custody of their underage children, born in wedlock, which of the parents, and to what degree, will cover the cost of upkeeping the children, and whether the husband is obliged, and to what degree, to provide maintenance to his divorced wife.

9. In default of agreement the question of the husband's participation in maintaining his wife, if she is disabled and has insufficient or no means of her own, and the question of adjudging custody of the children are decided as a common law case by the local court, regardless of the amount in controversy. After decreeing, personally and on the spot, the marriage dissolved the judge passes an interim decision on the destiny of the children and decides the question of temporary maintenance of both the children and the wife, if she is in need of such.

10. Henceforth it shall be within the competence of the local courts to declare marriages illegal or invalid.

11. This law applies to all citizens of the Russian Republic regardless of their religion.

12. All divorce cases now before the consistories of the Orthodox and other religious denominations, the Synod Directing, the various institutions of other Christian and non-Christian denominations, and officials of clerical institutions of all denominations, on which decisions have not been passed or, having been passed, have not acquired legal force yet, are declared, in virtue of this law, annulled, and their records, together with all the records of the divorce cases that have been handled by these institutions and officials, are to be handed over forthwith for keeping to the district courts. The parties in such cases may, without waiting for their discontinuance, hand in new applications for the dissolution of marriage under the present decree, without having to renew the publication as specified in Paragraphs 4 and 5.

Chairman of the Central Executive Committee of Soviets of Workers', Soldiers' and Peasants' Deputies, Y. SVERDLOV.
Chairman of the Council of People's Commissars, V. ULYANOV (LENIN).

Business Manager of the Council of People's Commissars, BONCH-BRUYEVICH.
Secretary, N. GORBUNOV.

Decrees, Vol. 1, pp. 237–239.

23. DECREE OF THE COUNCIL OF PEOPLE'S COMMISSARS ON THE EQUALIZATION OF RIGHTS OF ALL SERVICEMEN[18]

December 29 (16), 1917

Implementing the will of the revolutionary people for the speediest and resolute elimination of all vestiges of inequality in the army, the Council of People's Commissars resolves:

(1) All ranks and grades in the army, from corporal to general, are hereby abolished. The army of the Russian Republic will henceforth consist of free and equal citizens bearing the honorary name of soldiers of the revolutionary army.

(2) All privileges accruing from the former ranks and grades, as well as all insignia, are abolished.

(3) All titling is abolished.

(4) All decorations and other signs of distinction are abolished.

(5) With the abolition of the officer's grade all exclusive officers' organizations are dissolved.

(6) The institution of orderlies in the army in the field is abolished.

NOTE. Orderlies remain only in the regimental offices, committees and other army organizations.

Chairman of the Council of People's Commissars, V. ULYANOV (LENIN).
People's Commissar for the Affairs of the Army and Navy, N. KRYLENKO.
People's Commissar for Military Affairs, PODVOISKY.
Assistants of the People's Commissar for Military Affairs, KEDROV, SKLYANSKY, LEGRAN, MEKHONOSHIN.
Secretary of the Council, N. GORBUNOV.

December 16, 1917.

Decrees, Vol. 1, p. 243.

24. DECREE OF THE COUNCIL OF PEOPLE'S COMMISSARS ON ELECTIVITY AND ORGANIZATION OF AUTHORITY IN THE ARMY[19]

December 29 (16), 1917

(1) The Army, which serves the will of the working people is subordinated to the spokesman of this will, the Council of People's Commissars.

(2) All power in the units and their formations is vested in the respective soldiers' committee and Soviets.

(3) Those areas of the life and activity of troops which are already within the competence of the committees will henceforth be under their direct authority. Those areas of activity guidance of which cannot be assured by the committees are placed under the control of the committees or Soviets.

(4) Election of command personnel and officials is hereby introduced. Commanders up to regimental level are elected at general meetings of their squads, platoons, companies, teams, squadrons, batteries, battalions and regiments. Commanders of higher than regimental level, up to the supreme commander-in-chief, are elected by congresses or conferences convened by the respective committees.

NOTE: Conference is to be understood as a session of the respective committee jointly with delegates from committees standing one rank lower.

(5) Elected commanders of a level higher than regimental are approved by the committee standing one rank higher.

NOTE: In the event of a substantiated refusal of the higher committee to approve an elected commander, a commander elected by the lower committee a second time is subject to obligatory approval.

(6) Commanders of armies are elected by army congresses. Front commanders are elected by congresses of fronts.

(7) Only those persons who have appropriate technical knowledge are assigned by the respective committees of special units to posts requiring special education, special knowledge or other practical training, such as doctors, engineers, technicians, telegraph operators, radiotelegraph operators, aeronauts, automobilists, etc.

(8) Chiefs of staff are elected by congresses from among persons with special training.

(9) All other staff members are appointed by chiefs of staff and approved by respective congresses.

NOTE: All persons with a special education are to be registered separately.

(10) The right to retire is granted to members of the command personnel of an age higher than the call-up age of soldiers who have not been elected to some or other posts and have been thereby reduced to the position of privates.

(11) Appointments to all non-command posts, with the exception of those in the supply service, are made by the elected commander concerned.

(12) Detailed instructions regarding the election of command personnel will be issued separately.

Chairman of the Council of People's Commissars, V. ULYANOV (LENIN).
People's Commissar for the Affairs of the Army and Navy, N. KRYLENKO.
People's Commissar for Military Affairs, PODVOISKY.
Assistants of the People's Commissar for Military Affairs, KEDROV, SKLYANSKY, LEGRAN, MEKHONOSHIN.
Secretary of the Council, N. GORBUNOV.

December 16, 1917.

Decrees, Vol. 1, pp. 244–245.

25. DECREE OF THE ALL-RUSSIA CENTRAL EXECUTIVE COMMITTEE AND THE COUNCIL OF PEOPLE'S COMMISSARS ON CIVIL MARRIAGE, ON CHILDREN AND ON THE KEEPING OF REGISTERS

December 31 (18), 1917

The Russian Republic will henceforth recognize only civil marriage.

Civil marriage is consummated in keeping with the following rules:

1. Persons wishing to enter into marriage declare their intention verbally or hand in an application to that effect to the registry office of the local (city, district, *uyezd* or *volost*) self-government body.

NOTE. A religious ceremony, performed in addition to the obligatory civil wedding, is a private affair of the persons concerned.

2. Marriage applications will not be accepted from: (*a*) males under 18 and females under 16. In Transcaucasia the native population can marry upon the attainment of the age of 16 by the bridegroom and 13 by the bride; (*b*) relatives in the direct line, full and half brothers and sisters, with consanguinity recognized also between a natural child and his descendants, on one side, and his father and his relatives, on the other; (*c*) married persons; (*d*) insane persons.

3. Persons wishing to enter into marriage present themselves at the registry office and make written statements as to the absence of obstacles to marriage indicated in Paragraph 2 and to the effect that they marry of their own free will.

Persons knowingly making false statements as to the absence of obstacles enumerated in Paragraph 2 are prosecuted for perjury, and their marriage in invalidated.

4. Upon taking these statements the head of the marriage registration department enters the fact of conclusion of marriage upon the marriage register and proclaims the marriage consummated.

The newlyweds are free to decide whether they will henceforth bear the family name of the husband or of the wife or a combined family name.

In witness of the conclusion of marriage the newlyweds are forthwith issued a copy of their marriage certificate.

NOTE. A model form of the marriage register is appended.

5. Complaints against refusal to register marriage or against incorrect registration are lodged, without limitation of time, with the local judge, whose decisions on such complaints can be complained against in the established order.

6. In the event of the old registers having been destroyed or ceased to exist in any other way, or of the married couple being unable for any other reason to obtain official confirmation of their conjugality they can hand in an application to the registry office at the place of their residence or of the residence of one of them, to the effect that they have been married since such-and-such a time, This application, supplemented with a written statement as indicated in Paragraph 4 and a written statement to the effect that the register has really been destroyed or that they cannot for some other valid reason obtain a confirmation of their marriage, serves as the basis for a new registration of their marriage and the issue of a copy of the certificate.

CHILDREN

7. The birth of a child is registered by the registry office at the place of residence of the mother, with every birth registered separately.

NOTE. A model form of the birth register is appended.

8. Declaring the birth of a child to the registry office is the duty of its parents or one of them, or of the persons who take care of the child in view of the death of the parents, who also indicate the name and family name of the child and present two witnesses to attest to the fact of birth.

9. Two copies of marriage and birth registers are kept, with one copy deposited, after the expiration of every year, at the local court.

10. Children born out of wedlock are equalized in rights with children born in wedlock as regards the rights and duties of both the parents in respect of the children and of the children in respect of the parents.

Persons who have handed in a corresponding application

and made a written statement are registered as father and mother of the child.

Those found guilty of having knowingly given false information about facts relevant to the birth of a child are prosecuted for perjury, and the registration is invalidated.

Should the father of a child born out of wedlock fail to hand in the above-mentioned application, the mother, the guardian or the child himself has the right to prove paternity in legal form.

DEATHS

11. Deaths are registered by the local registry office in the death register.

NOTE. A model form of the death register is appended.

12. The death of a person is reported to the registry office by the judicial or administrative authorities or the persons in whose care the deceased person was.

13. The institutions in charge of cemeteries shall not obstruct civil funeral rites within cemetery boundaries.

14. All clerical and administrative institutions which have been responsible for the registration of marriages, births and deaths, regardless of the religious cults according to which the rites were performed, shall hand over the registers without delay to the respective city, *uyezd* and *volost* local government bodies for keeping.

Chairman of the Council of People's Commissars, V. ULYANOV (LENIN).
Chairman of the Central Executive Committee of Soviets of Workers', Soldiers' and Peasants' Deputies, Y. SVERDLOV.
Business Manager of the Council of People's Commissars, BONCH-BRUYEVICH.
Secretary, N. GORBUNOV.

December 18, 1917.

Decree, Vol. 1, pp. 247–249.

26. DECREE ON STATE INDEPENDENCE FOR FINLAND, ISSUED BY THE COUNCIL OF PEOPLE'S COMMISSARS[20]

December 31 (18), 1917.

Responding to the Finnish Government's request for recognition of the independence of the Finnish Republic, the Council of People's Commissars, in full agreement with the principles of the right of a nation to self-determination, resolves:

To submit the following proposal to the Central Executive Committee:

(*a*) to recognize the state independence of the Finnish Republic

(*b*) to organize, in agreement with the Finnish Government, a special commission of representatives of both sides to elaborate practical measures stemming from Finland's secession from Russia.

Chairman of the Council of People's Commissars, V. ULYANOV (LENIN).
People's Commissars, I. SHTEINBERG, KARELIN, STALIN.
Business Manager of the Council of People's Commissars, BONCH-BRUYEVICH.
Secretary of the Council of People's Commissars, N. GORBUNOV.

December 18, 1917.

Decrees, Vol. 1, p. 250.

27. DECISION OF THE COUNCIL OF PEOPLE'S COMMISSARS ON ALLOWANCES FOR SCHOOLTEACHERS[21]

January 15 (2), 1918

Having heard the report of the People's Commissar of Public Education, the Council of People's Commissars has resolved, without anticipating the eventual decision on schoolteachers' salaries in 1918, to allocate to the Commissariat of Public Education 12,520,000 roubles for the issue of lump sums to ensure that every teacher receives an extra payment bringing his salary for November and December up to 100 roubles per month (i.e. 200 roubles in all).

Chairman of the Council of People's Commissars, VL. ULYANOV (LENIN).
People's Commissar of Public Education, A. V. LUNACHARSKY.
Business Manager of the Government, VLAD. BONCH-BRUYEVICH.
Secretary of the Council, N. GORBUNOV.

January 2, 1918.

Decrees, Vol. 1, p. 311.

28. DECREE OF THE ALL-RUSSIA CENTRAL EXECUTIVE COMMITTEE ON THE DISSOLUTION OF THE CONSTITUENT ASSEMBLY[22]

January 19 (6), 1918

At its very inception, the Russian revolution produced the Soviets of Workers', Soldiers' and Peasants' Deputies as the only mass organization of all the working and exploited classes capable of giving leadership to the struggle of these classes for their complete political and economic emancipation.

Throughout the initial period of the Russian revolution the Soviets grew in number, size and strength, their own experience disabusing them of the illusions regarding compromise with the bourgeoisie, opening their eyes to the fraudulence of the forms of bourgeois-democratic parliamentarism, and leading them to the conclusion that the emancipation of the oppressed classes was unthinkable unless they broke with these forms and with every kind of compromise. Such a break came with the October Revolution, with the transfer of power to the Soviets.

The Constituent Assembly, elected on the basis of lists drawn up before the October Revolution, was expressive of the old correlation of political forces, when the conciliators and Constitutional-Democrats were in power.

Voting at that time for candidates of the Socialist-Revolutionary Party, the people were not in a position to choose between the Right-Wing Socialist-Revolutionaries, supporters of the bourgeoisie, and the Left-Wing Socialist-Revolutionaries, supporters of Socialism. Thus the Constituent Assembly, which was to have crowned the bourgeois parliamentary republic, was bound to stand in the way of the October Revolution and Soviet power.

The October Revolution, which gave power to the Soviets and through them to the working and exploited classes, aroused frantic resistance on the part of the exploiters, and in putting down this resistance it fully revealed itself as the beginning of the socialist revolution.

The working classes learned through experience that old bourgeois parliamentarism had outlived its day, that it was utterly incompatible with the tasks of Socialism, and that only class insitutions (such as the Soviets) and not national ones were capable of overcoming the resistance of the propertied classes and laying the foundations of socialist society.

Any renunciation of the sovereign power of the Soviets, of the Soviet Republic won by the people, in favour of bourgeois parliamentarism and the Constituent Assembly would now be a step backwards and would cause a collapse of the entire October Workers' and Peasants' Revolution.

By virtue of generally known circumstances the Constituent Assembly, opening on January 5, gave the majority to the Party of Right-Wing Socialist-Revolutionaries, the party of Kerensky, Avsentyev and Chernov. Naturally, this party refused to discuss the absolutely precise, clear-cut and unambiguous proposal of the supreme body of Soviet power, the Central Executive Committee of the Soviets, to recognize the programme of Soviet power, to recognize the Declaration of Rights of the Working and Exploited People, to recognize the October Revolution and Soviet power. By doing so the Constituent Assembly severed all ties with the Soviet Republic of Russia. The withdrawal from such a Constituent Assembly of the groups of Bolsheviks and Left-Wing Socialist-Revolutionaries, who now are in an indisputably vast majority in the Soviets and enjoy the confidence of the workers and the majority of the peasants, was inevitable.

Outside the Constituent Assembly, the parties which have the majority there, the Right-Wing Socialist-Revolutionaries and the Mensheviks, are waging an open struggle against Soviet power, calling in their press for its overthrow and thereby objectively supporting the exploiters' resistance to the transition of land and factories into the hands of the working people.

Obviously, under such circumstances the remaining part of the Constituent Assembly can only serve as a cover for the struggle of the bourgeois counter-revolution to overthrow the power of the Soviets.

In view of this, the Central Executive Committee resolves:

The Constituent Assembly is hereby dissolved.

Decrees, Vol. 1, pp. 335–336.

29. DECLARATION OF RIGHTS OF THE WORKING AND EXPLOITED PEOPLE ADOPTED BY THE THIRD ALL-RUSSIA CONGRESS OF SOVIETS[23]

January 25 (12), 1918

I

(1) Russia is hereby proclaimed a Republic of Soviets of Workers', Soldiers' and Peasants' Deputies. All power, centrally and locally, is vested in these Soviets.

(2) The Russian Soviet Republic is established on the principle of a free union of free nations, as a federation of Soviet national republics.

II

Its fundamental aim being abolition of all exploitation of man by man, complete elimination of the division of society into classes, merciless suppression of the exploiters, socialist organization of society, and victory of socialism in all countries, the Third All-Russia Congress of Soviets of Workers', Soldiers' and Peasants' Deputies further resolves:

(1) Pursuant to the socialization of land, private land ownership is hereby abolished, and all land is proclaimed the property of the entire people and turned over to the working people without any redemption, on the principles of egalitarian land tenure.

All forests, mineral wealth and waters of national importance, as well as all live and dead stock, model estates and agricultural enterprises are proclaimed the property of the nation.

(2) The Soviet laws on workers' control and on the Supreme Economic Council are hereby confirmed in order to guarantee the power of the working people over the exploiters and as a first step towards the complete conversion of factories, mines, railways and other means of production and transportation into the property of the Soviet Workers' and Peasants' Republic.

The Third Congress of Soviets regards as a first blow at international banking, finance capital, the Soviet law on the annulment of loans negotiated by the governments of the tsar, the landlords and the bourgeoisie and expresses confidence that Soviet power will be advancing steadfastly along this road until the complete victory of an international workers' uprising against the rule of capital.

(3) The conversion of all banks into the property of the workers' and peasants' state is hereby confirmed as a prerequisite of the emancipation of the working people from the rule of capital.

(4) In order to eliminate parasitic sections of society, universal labour conscription is hereby instituted.

(5) To ensure the sovereign power of the working people and to rule out any possibility of restoration of the power of the exploiters, the arming of the working people, the creation of a socialist Red Army of workers and peasants, and the complete disarming of the propertied classes are hereby decreed.

III

Expressing firm determination to wrest mankind from the clutches of finance capital and imperialism, which have in this most criminal of wars drenched the world in blood, the Third Congress of Soviets unreservedly endorses Soviet policy of denouncing the secret treaties, organizing most extensive fraternization with the workers and peasants of the combatant armies and achieving at all costs by revolutionary means a democratic peace for the working people, without annexations of indemnities, on the basis of free self-determination of nations.

(2) With the same aim in view, the Third Congress of Soviets insists on a complete break with the barbarous policy of bourgeois civilization, which has built the prosperity of the exploiters in a few chosen nations through the enslavement of hundreds of millions of working people in Asia, in the colonies in general, and in small countries.

The Third Congress of Soviets supports the policy of the Council of People's Commissars which has proclaimed the complete independence of Finland, commenced the withdrawal of troops from Persia, and proclaimed freedom of self-determina-nation for Armenia.

IV

The Third All-Russia Congress of Soviets holds that now, in the hour of the people's resolute struggle against the exploiters, there should be no room for exploiters in any governmental agency. Power must belong fully and exclusively to the working people and their plenipotentiary representatives—the Soviets of Workers', Soldiers' and Peasants' Deputies.

At the same time, endeavouring to create a genuinely free and voluntary, and therefore all the more firm and stable union of the working classes of all the nations of Russia, the Third Congress of Soviets confines itself to promulgating the fundamental principles of a federation of Soviet republics of Russia, leaving it to the workers and peasants of each nation to decide independently at their own representative congresses of Soviets whether they wish to participate in the federal government and in the other federal Soviet Institutions, and on what terms.

Decrees, Vol. 1, pp. 341–343.

30. DECREE OF THE COUNCIL OF PEOPLE'S COMMISSARS ON THE PROTECTION OF ANTIQUES AND WORKS OF ART BELONGING TO THE POLISH PEOPLE

January 25 (12), 1918

Taking into consideration that objects of exceptional artistic or historical value to the Polish people, most of which were taken out of Poland before and during the retreat of Russian troops, are to be found in the western and north-western *gubernias* of the Russian Republic, in many towns and at country estates belonging to persons of Polish origin and with the aim of returning these objects intact to the entire Polish people, the Council of People's Commissars resolves and, as a guide to action for the revolutionary authorities concerned, announces the following:

1. Pending their transfer to Polish people's museums, antiques, objects of art, libraries, archives, paintings and rarities generally, wherever they may be found, are placed, as a national possession of the Polish people, under the protection of the Workers' and Peasants' Government as represented by the Commissariat for Polish Affairs and the Society for the Preservation of Antiques.

2. All articles are entered in deeds, with deeds of voluntary transfer of articles obtaining at Polish estates to Polish museums to be signed by the owners of these estates or by their attorneys. The deeds are drawn up in two copies, one for keeping at the Polish Commissariat of the Council of People's Commissars, and the other at the Petrograd branch of the Polish Society for the Preservation of Antiques, the official representative of the Polish artistic and historical societies.

3. In addition to the deeds, four copies of a detailed inventory of transferred objects are drawn up, with one copy to be retained by the owner, one by the Commissariat for Polish Affairs, one by the local commissariat for the preservation of antiques or the bureau of the nearest executive body of the Union of Polish Servicemen, and one by the board of the Society for the Preservation of Antiques in Petrograd.

4. The Polish Commissariat appoints special district com-

missars vested with powers of commissars of the Workers' and Peasants' Government to draw up deeds and inventories, carry into effect the present decree and supervise its implementation in the provinces.

5. All the above-mentioned organizations and persons shall work in contact with the local revolutionary authorities as represented by the local Soviets of Soldiers', Workers' and Peasants' Deputies, which are instructed to render all possible assistance in the preservation and transportation of Polish cultural values.

Chairman of the Council of People's Commissars, VL. ULYANOV (LENIN)
People's Commissar of Public Education, A. V. LUNACHARSKY
Commissar for Polish Affairs, Y. LESHCHINSKY
People's Commissar of the Interior, G. PETROVSKY
Business Manager of the Council of People's Commissars, V. BONCH-BRUYEVICH
Secretary of the Council, N. GORBUNOV

Decrees, Vol. 1, pp. 343–344.

31. RESOLUTIONS ON PEACE ADOPTED BY THE THIRD ALL-RUSSIA CONGRESS OF SOVIETS[24]

January 27 (14), 1918

(*Socialist-Revolutionaries*)

The Third All-Russia Congress of Soviets of Workers', Soldiers' and Peasants' Deputies, wholly approving the foreign policy of the Central Executive Committee and the Council of People's Commissars, hails all the steps of Soviet power designed to bring about an end to the worldwide carnage and establish a universal democratic peace.

The Third Congress voices complete confidence that further staunch defence of the Russian revolution's formula of peace will frustrate the overt annexationist designs of the German and Allied imperialists and lead to the complete triumph of the Russian socialist revolution.

The Third Congress, greeting the ever mounting revolutionary movement of the broad masses of working people in Austria–Hungary and other countries, firmly believes that the working class of the whole world will help the insurgent working people of Russia to end the war on principles undermining the rule of world imperialism, and will help to lead the whole of mankind, oppressed and bled white, on to the road of complete triumph of Socialism.

(*Bolsheviks*)

The All-Russia Congress of Soviets of Workers', Peasants' and Soldiers' Deputies confirms and approves all the statements and steps of Soviet power aimed at achieving a universal democratic peace.

The All-Russia Congress states that the terms laid down by the Austro–German delegation are not only a trampling underfoot of the principles of democracy but a complete repudiation of the principles the delegations of the Central Empires recognized in the declaration of December 12 (25).

The Central Empires are getting under their sway the Poles,

Lithuanians, half of the Latvians, part of the Ukrainians, Belorussians and Estonians and, depriving them of the right to genuine self-determination, are forcibly affirming in their midst the rule of the privileged and propertied upper crust. Thus the military occupation which the Central Empires intend to maintain even after the conclusion of universal peace is directly aimed against the implementation of a democratic peace on the principles proclaimed by the Russian revolution.

The All-Russia Congress expresses its firm belief that this annexationist policy (counter-revolutionary measures) will prove powerless to cut off the working people of Russia from the working people of Germany and Austria–Hungary.

In the powerful protest of the workers of Vienna, Lower Austria and Hungary against the annexationist peace, in the awakening revolutionary movement of the proletariat of Germany, the All-Russia Congress sees the best guarantee against an imperialist peace based on enslavement and coercion and camouflaged indemnity.

Proclaiming again for the whole world to hear the striving of the Russian people for an immediate termination of the war, the All-Russia Congress instructs its delegation to uphold the principles of peace stemming from the programme of the Russian revolution.

Long live an honest democratic peace!

Long live the revolutionary fraternity of the peoples!

Decrees, Vol. 1, pp. 348–350.

32. RESOLUTION OF THE THIRD ALL-RUSSIA CONGRESS OF SOVIETS ON THE FUNDAMENTALS OF THE FSFSR CONSTITUTION[25]

January 28 (15), 1918

(1) The Russian Socialist Soviet Republic is established on the basis of a voluntary union of the peoples of Russia, as a federation of the Soviet republics of these peoples.

(2) The supreme ruling body within the bounds of the federation is the All-Russia Congress of Soviets of Workers', Soldiers', Peasants' and Cossacks' Deputies, convened at least once in every three months.

(3) The All-Russia Congress of Workers', Soldiers', Peasants' and Cossacks' Deputies elects the All-Russia Central Executive Committee. The supreme body in the intervals between congresses is the All-Russia Central Executive Committee.

(4) The government of the federation, the Council of People's Commissars, is elected and dismissed from office, wholly or in part, by the All-Russia Congress of Soviets or the All-Russia Central Executive Committee.

(5) The manner of participation in the federal government of the Soviet republics, separate regions and regions with a distinct mode of living and national composition, as well as the spheres of activity of the federal and regional institutions of the Russian Republic are determined immediately upon the formation of regional Soviet republics by the All-Russia Central Executive Committee and the Central Executive Committees of these Republics.

(6) All local affairs are decided exclusively by the local Soviets. The higher Soviets are granted the right to regulate relations between the lower Soviets and to settle whatever disagreements may arise between them. It is a duty of the central Soviet authority to see to the observance of the fundamentals of the federation; it represents the Russian Federation of Soviets as a whole. The central authority is charged with the implementation of measures realizable only on a nationwide scale; this, however, should not involve violation of the rights of the individual regions that have joined the federation.

(7) The Central Executive Committee of Soviets is instructed to elaborate these fundamentals of the Constitution of the Russian Federative Republic and submit them to the next congress of Soviets.

Decrees, Vol. 1, pp. 350–351.

33. RESOLUTION OF THE THIRD ALL-RUSSIA CONGRESS OF SOVIETS ENDORSING THE NATIONALITIES POLICY ON THE SOVIET GOVERNMENT

January 28 (15), 1918

The All-Russia Congress of Soviets of Workers', Soldiers' and Peasants' Deputies hails and fully approves the nationalities policy of the Government of People's Commissars aimed at implementing the principle of self-determination of nations understood in the spirit of self-determination of the working people of all the nationalities of Russia. Specifically, the Congress of Soviets of Workers', Soldiers' and Peasants' Deputies endorses the decrees of the Council of People's Commissars and the Central Executive Committee on Finland and Armenia.

The Congress expresses its deep conviction that further steps of Soviet power in this direction will contribute to the transformation of the former Russian Empire, which kept the various nationalities within its confines by oppression and coercion, into a fraternal union of freely federated Soviet republics of Russia.

Decrees, Vol. 1, p. 351.

34. DECREE OF THE COUNCIL OF PEOPLE'S COMMISSARS ON THE ORGANIZATION OF THE WORKERS' AND PEASANTS' RED ARMY[26]

January 28 (15), 1918

The old army was an instrument of class oppression of the working people by the bourgeoisie. With the transition of power to the working and exploited classes there has arisen the need for a new army as the mainstay of Soviet power at present and the basis for replacing the regular army by the arming of the whole people in the near future, and as a support for the coming socialist revolution in Europe.

I

In view of the aforesaid, the Council of People's Commissars resolves to organize a new army, to be called the Workers' and Peasants' Red Army, on the following principles:

(1) The Workers' and Peasants' Red Army is built up from the most conscious and organized elements of the working people.

(2) Access to its ranks is open to all citizens of the Russian Republic who have attained the age of 18. Every one who is prepared to devote his forces, his life to the defence of the gains of the October Revolution, the power of the Soviets, and socialism can join the Red Army. Joining the ranks of the Red Army requires characteristics from army committees or democratic public organizations standing on the platform of Soviet power, Party or trade union organizations, or at least two members of these organizations. Joining by whole units calls for mutual guarantee and a signed vote.

II

(1) The Workers' and Peasants' Red Army soldiers are fully maintained by the State and receive, on top of that, 50 roubles monthly.

(2) Invalid members of the families of Red Army soldiers

who formerly were their dependants are provided with everything necessary according to the local consumer quotas, in keeping with the decisions of the local bodies of Soviet power.

III

The supreme authority for the Workers' and Peasants' Red Army is the Council of People's Commissars. Direct guidance and administration of the army is concentrated in the Commissariat of Military Affairs and the special All-Russia Board attached to it.

Chairman of the Council of People's Commissars, V. ULYANOV (LENIN)
Supreme Commander-in-Chief, N. KRYLENKO
People's Commissars for the Affairs of the Army and the Navy, DYBENKO and PODVOISKY
People's Commissars: PROSHYAN, ZATONSKY and SHTEINBERG
Business Manager of the Council of People's Commissars, VLAD. BONCH-BRUYEVICH
Secretary of the Council of People's Commissars, N. GORBUNOV

January 15, 1918.

Decrees, Vol. 1, pp. 356–357.

35. DECREE OF THE COUNCIL OF PEOPLE'S COMMISSARS ON FREEDOM OF CONSCIENCE AND ON CLERICAL AND RELIGIOUS SOCIETIES[27]

February 2 (January 20), 1918

1. The church is hereby separated from the state.

2. It is forbidden on the territory of the republic to issue any local laws or ordinances which would hamper or restrict freedom of conscience or would establish any advantages or privileges on account of the religion of citizens.

3. Every citizen is free to profess any religion or profess none. All deprivations of rights connected with the profession or non-profession of any religion are hereby abolished.

NOTE. Any indication of religious affiliation or non-affiliation of citizens shall be removed from all official acts.

4. The actions of state and other public-law social institutions shall not be accompanied by any religious rites or ceremonies.

5. Free performance of religious rites is guaranteed in so far as these do not violate public order and are not accompanied by violation of the rights of citizens or of the Soviet Republic.

The local authorities have the right to take all necessary measures to ensure, in such cases, public order and security.

6. No one can evade, on the plea of his religious views, performance of his civic duties.

In particular instances exceptions to this rule are allowed by decision of a people's court, on the condition of substitution of one civic duty for another.

7. The religious oath is abolished.

A solemn oath is given when necessary.

8. Civil registers are kept exclusively by the civil authority, namely, by marriage and birth registration departments.

9. The school is hereby separated from the church.

Religious instruction in all state, public and private educational establishments where general educational subjects are taught, is not allowed.

Citizens can teach and be taught religion privately.

10. All clerical and religious societies abide by the general

regulations concerning private societies and unions, enjoy no privileges and receive no subsidies from the state or from its local autonomous and self-governing institutions.

11. Compulsory subscriptions and levies in favour of clerical or religious societies, as well as measures of compulsion or punishment on the part of these societies with regard to their members, are not allowed.

12. No clerical or religious societies have the right to own property.

They have no rights of a juridical person.

13. All property of the clerical and religious societies existing in Russia is declared the property of the people.

Buildings and objects designed specifically for worship are handed over, by special decisions of the local or central state authority, to the religious societies concerned for free use.

Chairman of the Council of People's Commissars, V. ULYANOV (LENIN)
People's Commissars: N. PODVOISKY, V. ALGASOV, V. TRUTOVSKY, A. SHLIKHTER, P. PROSHYAN, V. MENZHINSKY, A. SHLYAPNIKOV, G. PETROVSKY
Business Manager, VL. BONCH-BRUYEVICH
Secretary, N. GORBUNOV

Decrees, Vol. 1, pp. 373–374.

36. DECREE OF THE ALL-RUSSIA CENTRAL EXECUTIVE COMMITTEE ON THE ANNULMENT OF STATE LOANS[28]

February 3 (January 21), 1918

1. All state loans negotiated by the governments of the Russian landlords and the Russian bourgeoisie, enumerated in a separately published list, are annulled as from December 1, 1917. The December coupons of these loans are not subject to payments.

2. All guarantees given by the aforesaid governments to various enterprises and institutions with regard to loans are likewise annulled.

3. All foreign loans are annulled unconditionally and without exception.

4. The short-term liabilities and series of the State Treasury remain in force. No interest is paid on them, their bonds remaining in circulation on a par with bank-notes.

5. Necessitous citizens holding annulled government bonds of internal loans to a sum not exceeding 10,000 roubles (at nominal value) are issued, in exchange, registered certificates of the new loan of the Russian Socialist Federative Soviet Republic to a sum not exceeding 10,000 roubles. The terms and conditions of the loan will be determined separately.

6. State savings bank deposits and interest on them are inviolable. All bonds of the annulled loans belonging to savings banks are replaced by the book debt of the Russian Socialist Federative Soviet Republic.

7. Cooperatives, local self-government bodies and other socially useful or democratic institutions holding bonds of the annulled loans are compensated in keeping with rules being worked out by the Supreme Economic Council jointly with representatives of these institutions, provided it has been proved that these bonds were purchased prior to the publication of this decree.

NOTE. It is within the discretion of the local agencies of the Supreme Economic Council to decide which local institutions fall within the category of socially useful or democratic.

8. General guidance in the annulment of state loans is entrusted to the Supreme Economic Council.

9. All practical matters related to the annulment of loans are entrusted to the State Bank, which is instructed to commence without delay the registration of all state loan bonds held by different owners, as well as other interest bearing securities, whether subject to annulment or not.

10. The Soviets of Workers', Soldiers' and Peasants' Deputies establish, by agreement with the local national economic councils, commissions to determine what citizens belong to the category of necessitous.

These commissions have the right completely to annul savings built up from unearned income, even if these savings do not exceed 5,000 roubles.

Chairman of the Central Executive Committee, Y. SVERDLOV

Decrees, Vol. 1, pp. 386–387.

37. DECREE OF THE COUNCIL OF PEOPLE'S COMMISSARS ON THE COUNCIL OF MEDICAL BOARDS[29]

February 6 (January 24), 1918

(1) The medical boards of all the People's Commissariats constitute the Council of Medical Boards.

(2) The Council of Medical Boards is the supreme medical agency of the Workers' and Peasants' Government.

(3) The Council of Medical Boards for medical and sanitary matters has a representative in the Council of People's Commissars in a consultative capacity.

Chairman of the Council of People's Commissars, V. ULYANOV (LENIN)
People's Commissars: PETROVSKY, TRUTOVSKY
Business Manager of the Government, BONCH-BRUYEVICH
Secretary of the Council, N. GORBUNOV

Decrees, Vol. 1, pp. 403–404.

38. DECREE OF THE COUNCIL OF PEOPLE'S COMMISSARS ON THE INTRODUCTION OF THE WEST-EUROPEAN CALENDAR[30]

February 6 (January 24), 1918

In order to establish the system of time-reckoning used by almost all cultured nations, the Council of People's Commissars resolves to introduce into civil life, after the expiry of the month of January of this year, a new calendar. In virtue of this:

(1) The first day after January 31, this year, shall be reckoned, not as February 1, but as February 14; the second day, as 15, and so on.

(2) The terms of all obligation, both contractual and under law, that would have fallen due, under the previous calendar, between February 1 and 14 of this year, shall be regarded as due between February 14 and 27, by adding 13 days to every respective date.

(3) The terms of all obligations that would have fallen due, under the previous calendar, between February 14 and July 1, this year, shall be regarded as due, given the agreement of both sides, 13 days later.

(4) The terms of all obligations that would have fallen due, under the previous calendar, beginning with July 1, this year, shall be regarded as due on the same dates also under the new calendar.

(5) In reckoning, on the first day after February 14 under the new calendar, the date of payment of interest on all state and private loans, dividend warrants, bank deposits and current accounts, 13 days shall be dropped from the time that has elapsed since the last payment of interest.

(6) Persons whose wages or salaries are paid at the end of every month shall receive, on February 28 of this year, their monthly pay minus $\frac{13}{30}$ of it.

(7) Persons whose wages or salaries are paid on the 15th and 30th of every month shall receive no pay on February 15 but shall receive, on February 20 of this year, their monthly pay minus $\frac{13}{30}$ of it.

(8) Persons whose wages or salaries are paid on the 20th of

every month shall receive, on February 20 of this year, their monthly pay minus $\frac{13}{30}$ of it.

(9) After January 31 of this year, the dates of payment of pensions and special allowances fixed in the relevant rules shall be reckoned as coming 13 days later.

(10) Until July 1 of this year, the date according to the heretofore effective calendar shall be indicated in brackets after the date according to the new calendar.

Chairman of the Council of People's Commissars, V. ULYANOV (LENIN)
Assistant People's Commissar of Foreign Affairs, CHICHERIN
People's Commissars: A. SHLYAPNIKOV, G. PETROVSKY, V. ALGASOV, V. OBOLENSKY
Secretary of the Council of People's Commissars, GORBUNOV

Decrees, Vol. 1, pp. 404–405.

39. REGULATIONS OF THE COUNCIL OF PEOPLE'S COMMISSARS ON LABOUR EXCHANGES[31]

February 9 (January 27), 1918

(1) For the purposes of (*a*) keeping accurate account of and ensuring planned distribution of manpower in all branches of the national economy; (*b*) regulating manpower supply and demand; (*c*) supervising persons drawing benefits under the unemployment insurance law, local and regional labour exchanges are instituted.

NOTE. Unemployed not registered at the local labour exchanges are not entitled to unemployment insurance benefits.

(2) Local labour exchanges are established by local trade union associations on the principles indicated hereinafter, to function under city or district authorities, in localities having not less than 20,000 residents.

In localities with less than 20,000 residents local labour exchanges can be set up by the Labour Exchanges Council on instructions from the trade unions or, where such do not exist, factory, agricultural or other workers' committees.

(3) The Labour Exchanges Council determine the area served by, and fixes the date of the opening of, a labour exchange.

NOTE. Pending the establishment of the Labour Exchanges Council the date of the opening of a labour exchange is determined by the People's Commissariat for Labour.

(4) In pursuance of the aims indicated in Paragraph 1, the local labour exchanges (*a*) register all persons who need a job and all the unemployed in the given locality; (*b*) register all instances of demand for manpower; (*c*) act as employment agencies; (*d*) keep statistical records of manpower supply and demand; (*e*) gather information about the situation on the local labour market; (*f*) organize canteens and hostels; (*g*) publish bulletins on the situation on the labour market; (*h*) organize on their premises, libraries, reading-rooms, etc.; (*i*) carry out other measures conducive to the implementation of the aims indicated in Paragraph 1.

(5) The local labour exchange is managed by a committee composed of representatives of the trade unions, two representatives of the local Soviet of Workers' Deputies, and two representatives of the city and district self-government.

NOTE. In the absence of trade unions, the committee includes representatives of factory, agricultural and other workers' committees.

(6) The expenses on the maintenance of local labour exchanges are defrayed by the city and district self-government, with a subsidy from the state the size of which is determined in every instance by the People's Commissariat for Labour.

(7) To unify and coordinate the activity of the local labour exchanges the Labour Exchanges Council institutes regional labour exchanges attached to the regional trade union associations.

(8) The services of the labour exchange are provided free of charge.

(9) The local and regional exchanges suspend their activities as employment agencies in respect of employers whose enterprises are involved in strikes.

(10) To coordinate the activity of the local and regional labour exchanges, an annual all-Russia congress of their representatives is convened, which institutes the leading body—the Labour Exchanges Council.

(11) The Labour Exchanges Council issues rules, instructions and explanations for the local and regional labour exchanges and unifies forms of filing, accounting and statistics.

(12) Pending the institution of the Labour Exchanges Council, the realization of the provisions set out in Paragraph 2 and 3 and in notes to Paragraphs 5, 7, 10 and 11 is the responsibility of the People's Commissariat for Labour.

(13) With regard to telegraph, telephone and postal communication, all labour exchanges enjoy the rights of government institutions.

(14) The regional and local labour exchanges established on the strength of the present Regulations enjoy the rights of a juridical person.

(15) With the enactment of these regulations all private employment agencies and other such establishments whose

purpose is to serve as intermediaries in providing employment for a fee or any other consideration, are prohibited.

(16) Factory and office workers are hired only through a labour exchange.

(17) Violation of Paragraph 15 incurs imprisonment for up to six months.

Chairman of the Council of People's Commissars, V. ULYANOV (LENIN)
People's Commissar of Labour, A. SHLYAPNIKOV, V. TRUTOVSKY
Business Manager of the Council of People's Commissars, V. BONCH-BRUYEVICH
Secretary of the Council of People's Commissars, N. GORBUNOV

Decrees, Vol. 1, pp. 424–426.

40. DECREE OF THE COUNCIL OF PEOPLE'S COMMISSARS ON THE ORGANIZATION OF THE WORKERS' AND PEASANTS' RED NAVY[32]

February 11 (January 29), 1918

The Russian navy, as well as the army, has been reduced by the crimes of the tsarist and bourgeois regimes and by the disasterous war to a state of extensive collapse, a circumstance which extremely complicates the transition to the arming of the people as demanded by the programme of the socialist parties. To safeguard the national property and to counter the remnants of the mercenary army of the capitalists and the bourgeoisie with an organized force, and also to support, in case of need, the ideas of the world proletariat, resort must be made, as a transitional measure, to the organization of the navy on the basis of recommendation of candidates by party, trade union and other mass democratic organizations.

In view of this, the Council of People's Commissars decrees:

The navy based on universal conscription under the tsarist laws is hereby proclaimed disbanded, and a Socialist Workers' and Peasants' Red Navy is organized.

The newspaper *Rabochaya i Krestyanskaya Krasnaya Armiya i Flot*, No. 12, January 31, 1918.

See also *Decrees*, Vol. 1, pp. 434–435.

41. DECREE NO. 2 ON THE JUDICATURE, ISSUED BY THE ALL-RUSSIA CENTRAL EXECUTIVE COMMITTEE AND THE COUNCIL OF PEOPLE'S COMMISSARS[33]

February 15, 1918

By way of amendment of the Decree on the Judicature dated November 24, 1917, the All-Russia Central Executive Committee of Soviets of Workers', Soldiers' and Peasants' Deputies resolves:

Part One

DISTRICT PEOPLE'S COURTS

1. To hear cases that go beyond the jurisdiction of local People's Courts, district People's Courts are instituted whose members are elected within each district by the local Soviets of Workers', Soldiers' and Peasants' Deputies. The districts remain the same as before, but the Soviets concerned may agree on changing the boundaries of the given district.

2. A general meeting of the district People's Court determines the number of civil and criminal departments, each consisting of a chairman and at least two permanent members. The number of members of the Court may be augmented or reduced by the local Soviets of Workers', Soldiers' and Peasants' Deputies at their own discretion or on the representation of judicial bodies.

The members of the Court elect from their midst the chairman of the court and the chairmen of the departments, recall them, if the need be, and elect others. Members of the Court, not excluding chairmen, are recalled by the Soviets that elected them.

3. All proceedings preparatory to a Court hearing are carried out collectively by at least three permanent members of the district People's Court. In the civil departments cases are heard by three permanent members of the district Court and four people's assessors. Criminal cases are heard by twelve alternate and two substitute assessors under the chairmanship of a permanent member of the Court.

The lists of people's assessors are drawn up by the *gubernia* and city Soviets of Workers', Soldiers' and Peasants' Deputies on the basis of lists of candidates presented by the district and *volost* Soviets.

The lists of alternate assessors to sit on every session are drawn up, by lot, by the executive committees of the Soviets.

NOTE. The size of the daily fees of assessors is determined by the same Soviets, bearing in mind the gradual obligatory transition to gratuitous performance by citizens of the state duty of administering justice.

Part Two

CASSATION OF DECISIONS

4. The right of appeal is abolished, and only cassation of decisions is allowed.

To examine cassation complaints against the decisions of district People's Courts on both civil and criminal cases the permanent members of the People's Courts elect from their midst, at a general meeting of the given region, an appropriate number of members of the regional People's Court who, in turn, elect from their midst the chairman of the regional court and the chairmen of its departments.

NOTE. Members of the regional Court can be recalled both by the Soviets that elected them to district courts and by the meeting that elected them to the regional Court.

5. In taking action on a cassation complaint the regional Court can reverse a decision not only in view of what it has found to be major violations of form but also if this decision is, in its judgement, obviously unjust.

Following the reversal the case is returned for retrial by a newly constituted Court. The Court of Cassation also has the right of pardon and mitigation of punishment.

NOTE. The Court may pass its judgement in the absence of either the plaintiff or prosecutor or the respondent or defendant, but only when it has been proved to the satisfaction of the Court that such absence has valid reasons.

Part Three

SUPREME SUPERVISORY AUTHORITY

6. To ensure the uniformity of the cassation practice of both the congresses of local judges and the regional People's Courts, a Supreme Supervisory Authority is instituted in Petrograd. Its members are elected by regional People's Courts for a term of not more than one year, and can be recalled by both regional courts and Soviets, and re-elected.

Finding contradictions in the interpretation of laws by different cassation instances, the Supreme Supervisory Authority hands down a unifying decision of principle, to serve the cassation instances as a guide to action.

Should an irremovable contradiction be found between a law in operation and the people's legal conscience, the Supreme Supervisory Authority makes a representation to the legislative bodies regarding the need for a new law.

Decisions of the Supreme Supervisory Authority can be disaffirmed only by the legislative body of Soviet power.

Part Four

LEGAL PROCEDURE AND COURT JURISDICTION

7. The hearing of arguments in Courts of all instances can be conducted in all local languages. The rules concerning the language of the hearing or proceedings are established by the Courts jointly with the Soviets of Workers', Soldiers' and Peasants' Deputies.

8. Both civil and criminal cases are heard according to the Court rules of 1864, in so far as such rules have not been abolished by decrees of the Central Executive Committee of Workers', Soldiers' and Peasants' Deputies and the Council of People's Commissars and do not run counter to the legal conscience of the working classes. If the Courts do not abide by obsolete or bourgeois laws, they state the reasons thereof in their judgements.

9. All matters of protective civil procedure, such as probate proceedings, adoption, etc., as well as matters connected with

matrimony and birth and generally all cases not requiring cash assessment, fall within the jurisdiction of local Courts. Bankruptcy cases involving sums of more than 3,000 roubles are triable by district People's Courts.

10. Questions of cognizability of both civil and criminal cases are decided, finally and without appeal, by the Court before which the case has been brought. Having found a case not under its jurisdiction, the Court immediately refers it, with all records, to what it regards as a properly qualified court, which is bound to decide the case.

11. Writs of execution on promissory notes, mortgage bonds and notarized letters of credit are issued, in keeping with the rules of compulsory execution, by notaries or persons acting in their capacity, who collect notary and other fees in the established amounts.

12. All formal challenges in civil procedure on the mixtion and fragmentation of actions and all restrictions on the sides in regard to the formal aspect of proceedings, visor presentation of new pleas and claims, counter-claims, extension of the case with new claims, joinder of new parties, etc., are abolished.

13. When hearing civil cases demanding special knowledge, the Court may, at its own discretion, invite experts to attend, and be heard at, Court sittings. The contending parties, too, have the right to invite, on agreement between themselves, equal numbers of experts. If one side declares its candidate but the other side fails to do so by the specified time, the Court may accept the nominated candidate and appoint an expert for the other side, or reject the nomination and appoint experts for both sides.

14. In respect of evidence the Court is not restricted by any formal considerations and is free to decide, depending on the circumstances of the case, whether to accept this or that evidence. Before testifying witnesses are warned about responsibility for false testimony. Taking an oath is abolished.

The privacy of books of account and other books is abolished, and it is within the discretion of the Court to demand the presentation of such books in keeping with the rules established for other written evidence.

15. The cases of state and public institutions are heard on

an equal footing with those of private individuals. Litigation between state institutions is not allowed.

16. Should a civil action be brought during a criminal proceeding, it is transferred, immediately after the question of punishment has been decided, to an appropriate civil Court, to be considered fully in keeping with the rules of civil procedure. But is it the duty of the criminal Court promptly to give effect to the action.

17. Prosecution and imprisonment of persons of either sex who have not reached the age of 17 is abolished. The cases of juveniles guilty of socially-dangerous deeds are examined by Commissions for Juveniles composed of representatives of departments concerned with justice, public education and welfare.

Part Five

COURT TAX AND LEGAL EXPENSES

18. Civil, criminal and arbitration Courts impose a tax on all civil suits if the sum in dispute exceeds 100 roubles. Pending a special decree, sums of 100 to 3,000 roubles are assessed at 2 per cent, those of 3,000 to 100,000 roubles, at 3 per cent, and those of more than 100,000 roubles, at 4 per cent, it being within the discretion of the Court, upon satisfying itself as to the insufficiency of the means of the plaintiff, to defer payment of the tax, but not till after the moment of exaction of the amount of judgement. In the same order the Court can also defer payment of all other legal costs.

19. Along with passing judgement on a civil suit the Court awards costs to the winning party. Instead of the present remuneration for the conduct of the case, the losing party may by adjudged to pay up to 10 per cent of the awarded or rejected sum in dispute, a part of which amount the court awards, at its discretion, to the winning party and converts the remainder into state revenue.

20. The collection of the cassation deposit is abolished. Instead, a non-returnable Court tax is paid as for a Court of primary jurisdiction. The order of calculation of cassation expenses remains unchanged.

Part Six

PRELIMINARY INVESTIGATION

21. Preliminary investigation of criminal cases that are beyond jurisdiction of local Courts is conducted by commissions of inquiry consisting of three persons elected, pending direct elections, by the Soviets of Workers', Soldiers' and Peasants' Deputies. In the interest of investigation the commission of inquiry may request the cooperation of the Red Guard and the people's militia as well as all private individuals, officials and state and public institutions.

The commission of inquiry may restrict the participation of the defence at the stage of preliminary investigation if it finds this to be in the interest of ascertainment of the truth.

Complaints against the decisions of commissions of inquiry are lodged with the district People's Court.

22. In criminal cases the indictment is replaced by the decision of the commission of inquiry on the institution of proceedings.

Should the district People's Court find this decision insufficiently substantiated it may return the case to the commission of inquiry, to be forwarded to one of the members of the Court.

Part Seven

PROSECUTION AND DEFENCE

23. Court examination is conducted with the participation of the prosecution and the defence.

24. Soviets of Workers', Soldiers' and Peasants' Deputies set up boards of persons who devote themselves to legal advocacy in the form of both public prosecution and public defence.

25. Members of these boards are elected and recalled by Soviets of Workers', Soldiers' and Peasants' Deputies. Only these persons can appear in Courts for a fee.

26. The Court can invite a member of the board to act as the public prosecutor in every case before it.

27. Should the accused fail, for some reason or other, to

use his right to invite counsel for the defence the Court provides him, at his request, with assistance through the agency of the aforesaid board of attorneys.

28. In addition to the above-mentioned prosecutors and defence attorneys, one prosecutor and one defence attorney from among those present at the sitting can take part in the debate.

Part Eight

PEOPLE'S ASSESSORS AND COURT EXAMINATION

29. People's assessors participate in court examination and have the right at any time throughout the trial to challenge the presiding judge appointed for the given sitting.

People's assessors decide the question of not only the fact of offence but also of the measure of punishment; it is within their competence to mitigate the punishment envisaged by law, down to the conditional or absolute discharge of the accused.

30. The presiding judge's final address is abolished. He only makes a statement as to the measures of punishment envisaged by law. The presiding judge takes part in the people's assessors' deliberations with the right of voice but no vote.

Part Nine

COMPLAINTS, PARDON AND RESTORATION TO RIGHTS

31. No complaints against acquittal, mitigated sentences or absolute discharge are allowed.

32. All persons condemned by a people's Court can petition the local People's Court for a conditional or pre-schedule release, pardon or restoration to rights. Having satisfied itself that the petition is not without serious foundation, this court refers the case to the court of original jurisdiction.

33. In regard to all judgements passed by Courts between October 25, 1917 and the entry of the present decree into

force, the sides have the right to demand a retrial by the same instance.

34. The time limit for the lodging of complaints, both by way of cassation and by private action, in all criminal and civil cases is one month. The lodging of a complaint stays execution only after a corresponding decision of the first or cassation instance.

Part Ten

EXECUTION OF JUDGEMENTS

35. Pending a special decree on elected executive bodies execution of judgements is performed in the order that has been effective until now, with members of the militia replaced, wherever possible, by Red Guards.

Part Eleven

LAWS NOW IN OPERATION

36. In trying civil and criminal cases the Court is guided by still operative laws only in so far as these have not been annulled by decrees of the Central Executive Committee and the Council of People's Commissars and do not contradict socialist legal conscience. Without limiting itself to formal law but always proceeding from considerations of justice, the court can overrule any reference to statutory limitation and, despite these or other objections of a formal character, award an obviously just claim.

The same justice shall be applied in the criminal Court.

Part Twelve

GENERAL PROVISIONS

37. The initial delimitation of boundaries for regional people's courts, determination of the number of members to be elected to these Courts and to the Supreme Supervisory Authority, and convocation of their first sessions are entrusted to the People's Commissariat of Justice.

In the future the manner of their procedure will be decided upon by them independently.

38. Judgements and sentences are passed by the new Courts in the name of the Russian Socialist Federative Soviet Republic.

39. Former officials of Courts of all instances and designations can be elected by Soviets of Workers', Soldiers' and Peasants' Deputies to new judicial and investigation institutions.

Chairman of the All-Russian Central Executive Committee of Soviets of Workers', Soldiers', Peasants' and Cossacks' Deputies,
YA. SVERDLOV
Chairman of the Council of People's Commissars, VL. ULYANOV (LENIN)
Business Manager of the Council of People's Commissars, VL. BONCH-BRUYEVICH
Secretary of the Council, N. GORBUNOV

Decrees, Vol. 1, pp. 466–474.

42. "THE SOCIALIST FATHERLAND IS IN DANGER!" DECREE OF THE COUNCIL OF PEOPLE'S COMMISSARS[34]

February 21, 1918

In order to save this exhausted and ravaged country from new ordeals of war, we decided to make a very great sacrifice and informed the Germans of our readiness to sign their terms of peace. Our truce envoys left Rezhitsa for Dvinsk in the evening of February 20 (7), and still there is no reply. The German Government is evidently in no hurry to reply. It obviously does not want peace. Fulfilling the task with which it has been charged by the capitalists of all countries, German militarism wants to strangle the Russian and Ukrainian workers and peasants, to return the land to the landowners, the mills and factories to the bankers, and power to the monarchy. The German generals want to establish their "order" in Petrograd and Kiev. The Socialist Republic of Soviets is in the gravest danger. Until the proletariat of Germany rises and triumphs, it is the sacred duty of the workers and peasants of Russia devotedly to defend the Republic of Soviets against the hordes of bourgeois-imperialist Germany. The Council of People's Commissars resolves:

(1) The country's entire manpower and resources are placed entirely at the service of revolutionary defence.

(2) All Soviets and revolutionary organizations are ordered to defend every position to the last drop of blood.

(3) Railway organizations and the Soviets associated with them must do their utmost to prevent the enemy from availing himself of the transport system; in the event of a retreat, they are to destroy the tracks and blow up or burn down the railway buildings; all rolling stock—carriages and locomotives—must be immediately dispatched eastward, into the interior of the country.

(4) All grain and food stocks generally, as well as all valuable property in danger of falling into the enemy's hands, must be

unconditionally destroyed; the duty of seeing that this is done is laid upon the local Soviets, and their chairmen are made personally responsible.

(5) The workers and peasants of Petrograd, Kiev, and of all towns, townships, villages and hamlets along the line of the new front are to mobilize battalions to dig trenches, under the direction of military experts.

(6) These battalions are to include all able-bodied members of the bourgeois class, men and women, under the supervision of Red Guards; those who resist are to be shot.

(7) All publications which oppose the cause of revolutionary defence and side with the German bourgeoisie, or which endeavour to take advantage of the invasion of the imperialist hordes in order to overthrow Soviet rule, are to be suppressed; able-bodied editors and members of the staffs of such publications are to be mobilized for the digging of trenches or for other defence work.

(8) Enemy agents, profiteers, marauders, hooligans, counter-revolutionary agitators and German spies are to be shot on the spot.

THE SOCIALIST FATHERLAND IS IN DANGER! LONG LIVE THE SOCIALIST FATHERLAND! LONG LIVE THE INTERNATIONAL SOCIALIST REVOLUTION!

Council of People's Commissars

February 21, 1918.
Petrograd.

Decrees, Vol. 1, pp. 490–491.

43. DECREE OF THE COUNCIL OF PEOPLE'S COMMISSARS ON THE RIGHT OF CITIZENS TO CHANGE THEIR FAMILY NAMES AND BYNAMES

March 4, 1918

(1) Every citizen of the Russian Soviet Federative Republic who has reached the age of 18 is free to change his family name or byname, in so far as this does not infringe upon the rights of third persons guaranteed by relevant laws.

(2) Persons wishing to change their family name or byname apply in person to the head of the local registry office and hand in an application and documents proving their identity or properly certified copies of these documents.

(3) The head of the registry office protocols the application, publishes it, at the applicant's expense, in the local government newspaper within two weeks, and simultaneously sends it for publication to the government newspaper of the central authority and notifies the institution keeping records of criminal convictions.

NOTE. The institution keeping records of criminal convictions is also charged with keeping records of changed names and their periodic publication.

(4) On the expiry of two months after the publication in the government newspaper of the central authority the person who has changed his or her name or byname has the right to demand that this name be entered into all civil registry acts.

(5) In the event of a family name or byname being changed by persons in the marital state the change applies to their children aged below 18.

(6) The spouses of persons changing their family names or bynames, and their children who have reached the age of 18 can, if they wish, assume the new names of their spouses or parents. They make a written statement of their consent or refusal, jointly with or independently of their spouses or parents, in the order indicated above.

Chairman of the Council of People's Commissars, VL. ULYANOV (LENIN).
Secretary of the Council, GORBUNOV.

Petrograd, March 4.

Decrees, Vol. 1, pp. 520–521.

44. RESOLUTION OF THE EXTRAORDINARY FOURTH ALL-RUSSIA CONGRESS OF SOVIETS ON RATIFICATION OF THE PEACE TREATY OF BREST-LITOVSK[35]

March 15, 1918

The Congress confirms (ratifies) the peace treaty signed by our representatives at Brest-Litovsk on March 3, 1918.

The Congress recognizes as correct the actions of the Central Executive Committee and the Council of People's Commissars in deciding to conclude the present incredibly harsh, rapacious and humiliating peace in view of our having no army and of the extreme war weariness of the people, who in their distress have received no support from the bourgeoisie and bourgeois intelligentsia, but have seen that distress made use of for selfish class purposes.

The Congress also recognizes the undoubted correctness of the actions of the peace delegation that refused to enter into a detailed discussion on the German peace terms, because those terms were imposed on us in the form of an obvious ultimatum and by undisguised force.

The Congress most resolutely poses before all workers, soldiers and peasants, all the working and oppressed masses the main and most urgent task of the moment—the enhancement of activity and self-discipline of the working people; the creation throughout the country of strong, well-founded organizations that cover, as far as possible, all production and distribution; the ruthless struggle against the chaos, disorganization and economic havoc which are historically inevitable as the legacy of a most agonizing war, but which, at the same time, present the main obstacle to the complete victory of Socialism and the strengthening of the foundations of socialist society.

Today, after the October Revolution, after the overthrow of the political power of the bourgeoisie in Russia, after our denunciation and publication of all secret imperialist treaties, after the cancellation of the foreign loans, after the Workers' and Peasants' Government has proposed a just peace to all peoples without exception, Russia, having escaped from the clutches of the imperialist war, has the right to announce that she is not a participant in the plunder and suppression of other countries.

The Russian Soviet Federative Republic, having unanimously condemned predatory wars, from now on deems it its right and its duty to defend the socialist fatherland against all possible attacks by any of the imperialist powers.

The Congress therefore deems it the primary duty of all working people to muster all forces to re-establish and increase the defence potential of our country, to re-establish its military strength on the basis of a socialist militia and the universal military training of all adolescents and adults of both sexes.

The Congress expresses its unswerving confidence that the Soviet Government, which has steadfastly adhered to the principles of international solidarity of the workers of all countries in their struggle for Socialism against capitalism, will continue to do everything possible to promote the international socialist movement, to secure and accelerate mankind's advancement along the road leading to emancipation from capitalism and wage slavery, to the creation of a socialist society and to an enduring, just peace for peoples.

The Congress is firmly convinced that the international workers' revolution is not far away and that the complete victory of the socialist proletariat is assured despite the fact that the imperialists of all countries do not hesitate to use the most brutal means to suppress the socialist movement.

Decrees, Vol. 1, pp. 532–535.

45. DECREE ON NATURALIZATION, ISSUED BY THE ALL-RUSSIA CENTRAL EXECUTIVE COMMITTEE[36]

April 1, 1918

The acquisition of Russian citizenship by aliens is determined by the following stipulations:

1. Every alien residing on the territory of the Russian Socialist Federative Soviet Republic can acquire the rights of Russian citizenship.

2. An alien wishing to become a naturalized Russian subject applies to the local Soviet of Workers', Soldiers', Peasants' and Cossacks' Deputies, stating his occupation and indicating whether he was prosecuted by a court of law on a criminal charge, and if so, for what offence.

3. The identity of the applicant, should there be no other way of ascertaining it, is attested to by full citizens of the Russian Socialist Federative Soviet Republic.

NOTE. Those found guilty of having knowingly given false information with the aim of acquiring the rights of Russian citizenship shall be prosecuted for perjury and can be denaturalized.

4. Having satisfied itself that the applicant conforms to the requirements of Clauses 1 and 3 of the present Decree, the Soviet issues him an appropriate naturalization certificate.

5. In exceptional cases the rights of Russian citizenship can be conferred on aliens staying outside the Russian Socialist Federative Soviet Republic. Applications of such aliens, addressed to the Chairman of the Central Executive Committee, are handed in by them directly or through the nearest diplomatic representative of the Russian Socialist Federative Soviet Republic, and are considered by the Central Executive Committee.

6. The Soviet of Workers', Soldiers', Peasants' and Cossacks' Deputies reports on aliens admitted by it to Russian citizenship to the Commissariat of the Interior, which registers them, publishes their lists for general information and notifies, through

the People's Commissariat of Foreign Affairs, the states whose citizenship rights they held.

Chairman of the All-Russian Central Executive Committee of Soviets of Workers', Soldiers', Peasants' and Cossacks' Deputies, Y. SVERDLOV.
Secretary of the Central Executive Committee, V. AVANESOV.

Decrees, Vol. 2, pp. 40–41.

46. RESOLUTION OF THE COUNCIL OF PEOPLE'S COMMISSARS PERTAINING TO THE PROCLAMATION OF THE UKRAINIAN REPUBLIC AN INDEPENDENT FEDERATIVE SOVIET REPUBLIC[37]

April 3, 1918

Taking note of the declaration of the Plentipotentiary Embassy of the People's Secretariat of the Ukraine and the resolution of the Second All-Ukraine Congress of Soviets of Workers', Peasants' and Soldiers' Deputies proclaiming the Ukrainian People's Republic an independent Federative Soviet Republic, the Council of People's Commissars extends warm fraternal greetings to the Workers' and Peasants' Government, the People's Secretariat and the Central Executive Committee of Soviets of workers', Peasants', and Soldiers' Deputies of the Ukraine.

Compelled by the difficulties, which were exhaustively characterized in the resolution of the Extraordinary Congress of Soviets in Moscow, to enter into an agreement in keeping with the peace treaty with the Central Powers and the Kiev Rada, the Soviet Government of Russia expresses its enthusiastic solidarity for the heroic struggle being waged by the working and exploited people of the Ukraine, who now constitute one of the vanguard detachments of the world social revolution.

The Council of People's Commissars expresses its unshakable confidence that the time is not far off when the revolutionary masses of the Ukraine, acting hand in hand with the proletariat and peasantry of Russia and supported by the revolutionary socialist proletariat the world over, will triumph in the struggle against imperialist and capitalist oppression, for the complete emancipation of the working class and for Socialism.

Decrees, Vol. 2, p. 51.

47. DECREE OF THE ALL-RUSSIA CENTRAL EXECUTIVE COMMITTEE ON THE NATIONAL FLAG OF THE RUSSIAN REPUBLIC

April 8, 1918

The national flag of the Russian Republic is the Red Banner with the inscription, "Russian Socialist Federative Soviet Republic".

Chairman of the All-Russia Central Executive Committee, Y. SVERDLOV.
Secretary of the All-Russia Central Executive Committee, V. AVANESOV.

Decrees, Vol. 2, p. 62.

48. DECREE ON CONSUMERS' COOPERATIVES, ISSUED BY THE ALL-RUSSIA CENTRAL EXECUTIVE COMMITTEE AND THE COUNCIL OF PEOPLE'S COMMISSARS[38]

April 11, 1918

1. The consumers' cooperative organizations cater for all residents in the locality within the area of their operation.

All trading enterprises which supply the population with consumer goods pay to the state a special tax equalling 5 per cent of their turnover. Members of the consumers' societies are exempted from this tax, being refunded by their cooperatives, upon endorsement of the annual report, to the extent of 5 per cent of what they have been taking on account.

2. Persons short of means but wishing to join a consumers' society pay a minimum admission fee (not more than 50 kopecks). The membership fees of such persons can be built up from deductions from a 5 per cent tax on the goods taken by them.

NOTE. The method of verification of statements regarding shortage of means is determined by the local Soviets of Workers' Soldiers' and Peasants' Deputies.

3. Every definite district or locality is served by a definite consumers' society and its branches.

4. Not more than two consumers' cooperatives—one open to all citizens and the other for the working class one—can operate within the boundaries of any locality or territorial unit.

5. The standards of distribution of foodstuffs, etc., established by central or local Soviet government bodies, specifically by supply agencies, are obligatory both for private trading establishments and for cooperative organizations.

6. Representatives of unions of consumers' societies participate in the work of the central and local state supply agencies which exercise control over private trading establishments, and have the right to place them under management by the state.

NOTE. Consumers' societies placed by the cooperative centres on the same footing as cooperative unions enjoy the rights of such unions.

7. Owners and heads of trading and industrial enterprises of

a private-capitalist nature cannot be members of boards of consumers' societies.

8. Cooperative organizations which have united the entire population in their localities (see Paragraph 4) will be granted tax exemptions, to be defined separately.

9. The methods of implementing the present provisions are determined by cooperative organizations under the guidance of state supply agencies.

10. In measure as the cooperatives are provided with goods they begin to issue to the working population documents certifying the right to obtain definite consumer goods from them.

11. The Commissariat for Food Supply determines, in agreement with the Supreme Economic Council, both the forms and dates of presentation of accounts of cooperative societies and the forms of supervision and control over the cooperative and private trading establishments, in particular over the payment by them of the 5 per cent turnover tax to the state.

12. The consumers' societies give the Soviet Government every assistance in ensuring that all cash and working assets of both private owners and institutions be deposited in the State Bank, and carry out this measure in respect to their cash and working assets immediately upon the establishment, jointly with the Commissariat of Finance, of the necessary guarantees and privileges ensuring them free disposal of the means belonging to them.

13. Conformably with the development of the technical and economic apparatus of the unions of consumers' societies, the organs of Soviet power secure their participation in the purchase, procurement, processing and output of products, doing so on instructions from, with the assistance and under the control of, state supply agencies and the Supreme Economic Council.

Chairman of the Council of People's Commissars, VL. ULYANOV (LENIN).

Decrees, Vol. 2, pp. 91–92.

49. DECISION OF THE COUNCIL OF PEOPLE'S COMMISSARS ON THE EXPLORATION OF THE COUNTRY'S NATURAL WEALTH BY THE ACADEMY OF SCIENCES[39]

April 12, 1918

Having heard, at a sitting of April 12 this year, the report of the People's Commissar of Public Education on the Academy's offer of scientific services to the Soviet power in exploring the natural wealth of the country, the Council of People's Commissars resolved: to take a positive view of this offer, to recognize, in principle, the need for financing the relevant work of the Academy, and to pose before it the important and urgent task of achieving a correct distribution of industry in the country and the most rational utilization of its economic reserves.

Decrees, Vol. 2, p. 94.

50. DECREE ON MONUMENTS OF THE REPUBLIC, ISSUED BY THE COUNCIL OF PEOPLE'S COMMISSARS[40]

April 12, 1918

In commemoration of the great upheaval that has transformed Russia, the Council of People's Commissars resolves:

(1) Monuments erected in honour of Tsars and their servitors, which have neither historical nor artistic value, shall be removed from squares and streets; some of them to be placed in storehouses and others used for utilitarian purposes.

(2) A special commission, consisting of the People's Commissars concerned with public education and the property of the Republic and the head of the Fine Arts Department of the Commissariat of Public Education, is instructed to determine, in agreement with the Moscow and Petrograd Board of Arts, which monuments are to be removed.

(3) The same commission is instructed to mobilize artistic forces and organize a broad competition of projects of monuments to commemorate the great days of the Russian socialist revolution.

(4) The Council of People's Commissars expresses the wish that already on May Day some of the uglier idols be dismounted and the first models of new monuments put up for the masses to pass their judgement on them.

(5) The same commission is instructed speedily to prepare the May Day decoration of the city and the replacement of inscriptions, emblems, names of streets, coats of arms, etc. by new ones, expressive of the ideas and sentiments of revolutionary working Russia.

(6) The regional and *gubernia* Soviets shall act likewise, invariably in agreement with the aforesaid commission.

(7) The necessary sums shall be allocated as estimates are drawn up and are approved.

Chairman of the Council of People's Commissars, V. ULYANOV (LENIN).
People's Commissars: A. LUNACHARSKY, STALIN.
Secretary of the Council, GORBUNOV.

Decrees, Vol. 2, pp. 95–96.

51. DECREE ON COMPULSORY MILITARY TRAINING, ISSUED BY THE ALL-RUSSIA CENTRAL EXECUTIVE COMMITTEE[41]

April 22, 1918

One of the main objects of Socialism is to deliver mankind from the burden of militarism and from the barbarity of bloody clashes between nations. The goal of Socialism is universal disarmament, eternal peace and fraternal cooperation of all the peoples inhabiting the earth.

This goal will be achieved when power in all the strongest capitalist countries passes into the hands of the working class, which will wrest the means of production from the exploiters, turn them over to all working people for common use, and establish a Communist system as the unshakable foundation of the solidarity of all mankind.

At the present time it is in Russia alone that state power belongs to the working class. In all the other countries the imperialist bourgeoisie is at the helm. Its policy is aimed at suppressing the communist revolution and enslaving all weak nations. The Russian Soviet Republic, surrounded on all sides by enemies, has to create its own powerful army to defend the country, while engaged in remaking its social system along communist lines.

The Workers' and Peasants' Government of the Republic deems it its immediate task to enlist all citizens in universal labour conscription and military service. This work is meeting with stubborn resistance on the part of the bourgeoisie, which refuses to part with its economic privileges and is trying, through conspiracies, uprisings and traitorous deals with foreign imperialists, to regain state power.

To arm the bourgeoisie would mean to generate constant strife within the army, thereby paralysing its strength in the fight against the external enemies. The parasitic and exploiter elements who do not want to assume the same duties and rights as others cannot be given access to arms. The Workers' and Peasants' Government will find ways of making the bourgeoisie share, in some form or other, the burden of defending the Republic, upon which the crimes of the propertied classes have brought unheard-of trials and calamities. But in the immediate transitional period military training and arms will be given only to workers and to peasants who do not exploit the labour of others.

Citizens of 18 to 40 years of age who have undergone compulsory military training will be registered as subject to military service. At the first call of the Worker's and Peasants' Government they will have to take up arms and join the ranks of the Red Army, which consists of the most devoted and selfless fighters for the freedom and independence of the Russian Soviet Republic and for the international socialist revolution.

1. Military training is compulsory for the citizens of the Russian Soviet Federative Republic of the following ages: (1) school age, whose youngest limit is determined by the People's Commissariat of Public Education; (2) preparatory age, from 16 to 18 years, and (3) call-up age, from 18 to 40 years.

Female citizens are trained, with their consent, on an equal footing with males.

NOTE. Persons whose religious convictions do not allow the use of arms are trained only in those duties which do not involve the use of arms.

2. Training of persons of the preparatory and call-up ages is entrusted to the People's Commissariat for Military Affairs, and that of the school-age category to the People's Commissariat for Public Education, with the closest cooperation of the Commissariat for Military Affairs.

3. Military training is compulsory for workers employed in factories, workshops, at agricultural estates and in villages, and peasants who do not exploit the labour of others.

4. In the provinces compulsory military training is organized by area, *gubernia*, *uyezd* and *volost* military commissariats.

5. The trainees are in no way recompensed for the time spent in compulsory training; instruction shall be organized, as far as possible, in such a way so as not to divert the trainees from their normal permanent occupation.

6. Instruction shall be conducted continuously for eight weeks, at least 12 hours per week. The terms of training for special arms, and the procedure for refresher call-ups, will be determined in special regulations.

7. Persons who have been given training in the regular army

can be excused from compulsory training after passing an appropriate test, with the issue of certificates that they have undergone a course of compulsory training.

8. Instruction shall be given by trained instructors in accordance with a programme approved by the People's Commissariat for Military Affairs.

9. Persons who avoid compulsory training or neglect their duties stemming therefrom shall be called to account.

Chairman of the Central Executive Committee, Y. SVERDLOV.
Secretary, V. AVANESOV.

Decrees, Vol. 2, pp. 151–153.

52. DECREE OF THE COUNCIL OF PEOPLE'S COMMISSARS ON THE NATIONALIZATION OF FOREIGN TRADE[42]

April 22, 1918

I

All foreign trade is hereby nationalized. Transactions with foreign states and with individual foreign trading establishments on the purchase or sale of all kinds of produce (of the extractive and manufacturing industries, agriculture, etc.) are concluded in the name of the Russian Republic by specially authorized bodies. All import and export transactions in circumvention of these bodies are forbidden.

NOTE. Rules covering the movement of mail parcels and passenger luggage across the borders of the country will be issued separately.

II

The body in charge of nationalized foreign trade is the People's Commissariat for Trade and industry.

III

In order to organize import and export the People's Commissariat for Trade and Industry institutes the Council of Foreign Trade, to consist of representatives of the following authorities, institutions and organizations: (*a*) authorities concerned with military affairs, merchant marine, agriculture, transport, foreign affairs and finance; (*b*) central managerial bodies for individual branches of production, such as Centrochai (tea), Glavsakhar (sugar), Centrotextil, etc. and all the departments of the Supreme Economic Council; (*c*) central cooperative organizations; (*d*) central representative bodies of trading, industrial and agricultural organizations; (*e*) central bodies governing trade unions and the employees of trading and industrial organizations; (*f*) central bodies governing enterprises concerned with the import and export of most important items.

Note. The People's Commissariat for Trade and Industry has the right to include in the Council of Foreign Trade representatives of organizations not listed here.

IV

The Council of Foreign Trade implements the plan of foreign trade worked out by the People's Commissariat for Trade and Industry and approved by the Supreme Economic Council.

The functions of the Council of Foreign Trade include: (1) keeping record of the demand for and supply of exported and imported goods; (2) organization of procurement and purchase through branch centre (Glavsakhar, Glavneft, etc.) or, in their absence, through cooperatives and its own agencies and trading firms; (3) organization of purchase of foreign goods through state purchasing commissions and agents, cooperatives and trading firms; (4) fixing of prices for exported and imported commodities.

V

(1) The Council of Foreign Trade is divided into departments according to branches of production and the most important groups of exported and imported commodities, presided over by representatives of the People's Commissariat for Trade and Industry.

(2) A representative of the People's Commissariat for Trade and Industry is chairman of the general meeting of the Council of Foreign Trade and of its presidium, elected by the general meeting.

Note. The structure of the Council of Foreign Trade, the number of its departments, their functions, rights and sphere of activity will be determined separately.

(3) All decisions of the departments are submitted by the presidium of the Council for approval to the People's Commissariat for Trade and Industry.

VI

The present Decree enters into force from the moment of publication.

Chairman of the Council of People's Commissars, VL. ULYANOV (LENIN).
People's Commissars: GUKOVSKY, BRONSKY, STALIN, CHICHERIN.
Business Manager of the Council of People's Commissars, VL. BONCH-BRUYEVICH.
Secretary, N. GORBUNOV.

Moscow, April 22, 1918.

Decrees, Vol. 2, pp. 158–160.

53. DECREE OF THE COUNCIL OF PEOPLE'S COMMISSARS ON THE SUPPLY OF IMPLEMENTS AND METALS TO THE COUNTRYSIDE[43]

April 24, 1918

In order to regulate the supply of implements and metals to the countryside, and in pursuance of the decision of the Council of People's Commissars of November 30, 1917, declaring all domestically manufactured and imported machines and implements a monopoly of the Russian Federative Soviet Republic, the Council of People's Commissars resolves:

1. Development and testing of agricultural machines and implements, and all research as regards their application in different soil and climatic conditions, shall be conducted by the Commissariat for Agriculture.

2. Supervision over the manufacture of agricultural machines and implements and binder twine shall be transferred from the Commissariat for Food Supply to the Agricultural Engineering Section of the Metalworking Industry Department of the Supreme Economic Council.

3. All plants and workshops manufacturing agricultural machines and implements and binder twine, the tractor teams and workshop trains belonging to the Commissariat for Food Supply the Commissariat for Agriculture and other departments, together with their credits, allocations and current accounts, are placed at the disposal of the Agricultural Engineering Section of the Metalworking Industry Department of the Supreme Economic Council.

4. Organization of farm machinery production, elaboration of the plan of orders, and placement of orders within and outside the country is the exclusive jurisdiction of the Agricultural Engineering Section of the Supreme Economic Council.

5. The People's Commissariat for Agriculture shall keep records of the demand for agricultural machines and implements, binder twine and metals.

6. Plans for distribution of agricultural machines and implements, binder twine and metals required in agriculture are drawn up by the People's Commissariat for Agriculture and

approved by the same, along with the People's Commissariat for Food Supply and the Chairman of the Supreme Economic Council.

7. Agricultural machines and implements, binder twine and metals required in agriculture are distributed by and Commissariat for Food Supply and its agencies.

The guiding principle in distributing agricultural machines, etc. shall be, on the one hand and in the first place, to meet the interests of agricultural production, the interests of bringing all land under cultivation and raising the efficiency of agriculture, and, on the other hand, to supply agricultural machines, etc. first and foremost to the working and poorest part of the rural population, the common aim being to ensure the correct and adequate supply of bread to the entire population of the state.

Chairman of the Council of People's Commissars, V. ULYANOV (LENIN).
People's Commissars: A. TSYURUPA, G. CHICHERIN, I. GUKOVSKY.
Business Manager of the Council of People's Commissars, VL. BONCH-BRUYEVICH.
Secretary of the Council, N. GORBUNOV.

Decrees, Vol. 2, pp. 171–172.

54. DECREE ON THE ABOLITION OF INHERITANCE, ISSUED BY THE ALL-RUSSIA CENTRAL EXECUTIVE COMMITTEE[44]

April 27, 1918

I

Inheritance, both legal and testamental, is hereby abolished. After the death of an owner his property, personal and real, becomes public property of the Russian Socialist Federative Soviet Republic.

NOTE. The extinction and devolution of the right of use of agricultural plots is determined by rules laid down in the Basic Law on Land Socialization.

II

Pending the issue of a decree on universal social maintenance, the needy (i.e. living below the subsistence minimum) disabled direct descendant and ancestors, full and half brothers and sisters and spouse of the deceased person, receive maintenance from the property that belonged to him or her.

NOTE 1. No distinction is made between marital and extra-marital relationship.

NOTE 2. The relationship between adoptees and their progeny, on one side, and adopters, on the other, is regarded as that of consanguinity.

III

If the deceased person's property is insufficient to ensure the maintenance of the spouse and all other relatives as indicated in the previous section, priority is given to the neediest of them.

The size of the allowance to be paid to the spouse and other relatives out of the deceased person's property is determined by the social maintenance institution of the *gubernia* or, as in Moscow and Petrograd, city Soviets of Workers' and Peasants' deputies in agreement with the persons entitled to maintenance or, in the event of disagreement between them, by the local court through normal legal action. Suits of this kind fall within the jurisdiction of the Soviets of Workers' and Peasants' Deputies and the local courts at the deceased person's last place of residence.

V

All property of the deceased person, with the exception of that indicated in Section IX of the present Decree, comes under the authority of the local Soviet, which turns it over, in accordance with the deceased person's last place of residence or the location of this property, to the institution that manages the property of the Russian Republic.

VI

The local Soviet makes public the fact of the death of the owner of property for general information and invites persons entitled to maintenance out of this property to present themselves within a twelvemonth period.

VII

Persons failing to present their claims within the period indicated in the above section forfeit their right to maintenance out of the deceased person's property.

VIII

Expenses of administration are the first charge on the deceased person's property. The relatives and spouse of the deceased person receive maintenance out of his or her property in preference to creditors. Creditors whose claims have been found valid are satisfied out of the remaining property. Should this property prove insufficient to meet all their claims, general rules of bankruptcy proceedings are applied.

IX

The deceased person's property valued at not more than 10,000 roubles, specifically one consisting of a homestead, household furnishings and instruments of labour in town or countryside, comes under the direct administration and management of the spouse and relatives specified in Section II of the present Decree, if such are available. The order of administration and management is established by agreement between the aforesaid spouse and relatives or, failing this agreement, by the local court.

X

The present Decree is retroactive in regard to all property that became heritable prior to the publication of the present Decree, if the heirs have not acquired rights to it or, having acquired these rights, have not assumed possession of it yet.

XI

All probate cases at law, and probate proceedings generally, are discontinued, and the property in question is placed forthwith under the jurisdiction of the local Soviets or institutions specified in Section V of the present Decree.

NOTE. A special decision will be issued regarding estates indicated in Section IX of the present Decree which has become such prior to the publication of the Decree.

XII

The People's Commissariat for Justice shall publish, by agreement with the People's Commissariats for Social Maintenance and Labour, detailed instructions of giving effect to the present Decree.

The Decree enters into force from the day of signing and is given effect by telegraph.

Chairman of the Central Executive Committee, SVERDLOV.
Secretary of the Central Executive Committee, AVANESOV.

Decrees, Vol. 2, pp. 187–190.

55. INSTRUCTION OF THE PRESIDIUM OF THE CENTRAL EXECUTIVE COMMITTEE TO ALL SOVIETS TO BE GUIDED BY V. I. LENIN'S THESES ON THE IMMEDIATE TASKS OF THE SOVIET GOVERNMENT[45]

May 4, 1918

Having heard and discussed, at a sitting on April 19, 1918, Comrade Lenin's report on the immediate tasks of the Soviet Government, the All-Russia Central Committee unanimously approved the theses set forth by him. The final wording of the theses, upon which all Soviets are to base all their work, was entrusted to the Presidium of the Central Executive Committee jointly with the rapporteur. Having completed this mission, the Presidium communicates the following theses to all local Soviets, to serve them as a guide to action:

(1) The international position of the Soviet Republic is extremely difficult and critical, because the deep-rooted and fundamental interests of international imperialism induce it to strive not only for a military onslaught on Russia, but also for an agreement on the partition of Russia and the strangulation of Soviet power.

Only the stepping up of the imperialist slaughter of the peoples in Western Europe, and the imperialist rivalry between Japan and America in the Far East, paralyse or restrain these aspirations, and then only partially, and only for a certain, probably short, time.

Consequently the tactics of the Soviet Republic must be, on the one hand, to exert every effort to ensure the country's speediest economic recovery, to increase its defence capacity, and to build up a powerful socialist army; on the other hand, in international policy, the tactics must be those of manoeuvring, retreat, waiting for the moment when the international proletarian revolution—which is now maturing more quickly than before in a number of advanced countries—fully matures.

(2) In the sphere of domestic policy, the task that comes to the forefront at the present time, in conformity with the resolution adopted by the All-Russia Congress of Soviets on March 15, 1918, is the task of organization. It is this task, as

viewed in the context of the new and higher organization of production and distribution on the basis of socialized large-scale machine production, that constitutes the essence, and the chief condition for the complete victory, of the socialist revolution that was initiated in Russia on October 25 (November 7), 1917.

(3) From the purely political point of view, the crux of the present situation is that the task of convincing the working people of Russia that the programme of the socialist revolution is correct, and the task of winning Russia from the exploiters for the working people have, in main and fundamental outlines, been carried out, and the chief problem that comes to the forefront now is how to administer Russia. The organization of proper management, and the steady implementation of the decisions of the Soviet Government, constitute the urgent task of the Soviets and the vital condition for the complete victory of the Soviet type of state, which it is not enough to proclaim in formal decrees, which it is not enough to establish and introduce in all parts of the country, but which also must be practically organized and tested in the course of the regular, everyday work of administration.

(4) In the sphere of the economic building of Socialism, the crux of the present situation is that our work of organizing the country-wide comprehensive accounting and control of production and distribution, and of introducing proletarian control of production, lags far behind the direct expropriation of the expropriators—the landowners and capitalists. This is the fundamental fact determining our tasks.

From this it follows, on the one hand, that the struggle against the bourgeoisie is entering a new phase, i.e. the centre of gravity is shifting to the organization of control and accounting. Only in this way is it possible to consolidate all the economic achievements in the struggle against capital, and make secure all the measures in nationalizing individual branches of the national economy that we have carried out since October; only in this way is it possible to prepare for the successful consummation of the struggle against the bourgeoisie, i.e. the complete consolidation of Socialism.

From this basic fact follows, on the other hand, the explanation of why the Soviet Government was obliged in certain cases to take a step backward, or to agree to compromise with bourgeois tendencies. Such a step backward and departure from the principles of the Paris Commune was, for example, the introduction of high salaries for a number of bourgeois experts. Such a compromise was the agreement with the bourgeois cooperatives concerning steps and measures for gradually bringing the entire population into the cooperatives. Compromises of this kind will be necessary until the proletarian government has put country-wide control and accounting firmly on its feet; and our task is, while not in the least concealing their unfavourable features from the people, to exert efforts to improve accounting and control as the only means and method of completely eliminating all compromises of this kind. Compromises of this kind are needed at the present time as the sole guarantee of slower, but surer progress (because we are late with accounting and control). When accounting and control of production and distribution is fully introduced, the need for such compromises will be obviated.

(5) Particular significance is now attached to measures for improving labour discipline and raising labour productivity. Efforts already initiated in this field, especially by the trade unions, must be encouraged and redoubled. These include the introduction of the piece-work system, the adoption of what is scientific and progressive in the Taylor system, the payment of wages commensurate with the general results of the work of a factory, the operation of rail and water transport, etc. These also include the organization of competition between individual producers' and consumers' communes, selection of organizers, etc.

(6) The dictatorship of the proletariat is absolutely indispensable during the transition from capitalism to Socialism, and in our revolution this truth has been fully corroborated in practice. The dictatorship, however, presupposes a revolutionary government that is really firm and ruthless in crushing both exploiters and hooligans, but our government is too mild. Obedience during work, and unquestioning obedience at that, to the one-man decisions of Soviet directors, elected or appointed by Soviet institutions and vested with dictatorial powers (as is demanded, for example, by the railway decree), is far, very far, from being guaranteed as yet. This is due to the influence of the petty-

bourgeois element, the element of petty-proprietor habits, aspirations and sentiments, which fundamentally contradict proletarian discipline and Socialism. The proletariat must concentrate all its class-consciousness on the task of combating this petty-bourgeois element, which manifests itself both directly (in the support given by the bourgeoisie and their hangers-on, the Mensheviks. Right-Wing Socialist-Revolutionaries, etc. to every kind of resistance to the proletarian government), and indirectly (in the historical vacillation displayed by both the petty-bourgeois Left-Wing Socialist-Revolutionaries and the "Left Communist" trend in our Party, which descends to the methods of petty-bourgeois revolutionism and copies the Left-Wing Socialist-Revolutionaries).

Iron discipline and the thorough exercise of the dictatorship of the proletariat against petty-bourgeois vacillation—such is the general and summarizing slogan of the moment.

Chairman of the Central Executive Committee, SVERDLOV.
Secretary of the Central Executive Committee, AVANESOV.

Decrees, Vol. 2, pp. 228–231.

56. RESOLUTION ON V. I. LENIN'S REPORT ON FOREIGN POLICY, ADOPTED BY THE JOINT MEETING OF THE ALL-RUSSIA CENTRAL EXECUTIVE COMMITTEE AND THE MOSCOW SOVIET[46]

May 14, 1918

Having heard and discussed the report on foreign policy delivered by Comrade V. I. Lenin, Chairman of the Council of People's Commissars, the joint meeting of the All-Russia Central Executive Committee and the Moscow Soviet fully approves the policy of the Soviet Government, which is consistently implementing the decisions and instructions of the Extraordinary Fourth All-Russia Congress of Soviets.

The joint meeting considers that in the present extremely difficult and precarious situation the principal task of the Soviets is to step up efforts aimed at organizing a powerful Soviet Army, consolidating all organizations that unite the masses of workers and peasants, and cementing unity and discipline within these organizations.

In this trying period Soviet power should intensify dictatorship over the bourgeoisie.

Through the concerted, energetic work of all comrades truly devoted to the cause of the October Revolution, we will come, despite all obstacles, to the complete triumph of the world social revolution.

Decrees, Vol. 2, p. 267.

57. DECISION OF THE ALL-RUSSIA CENTRAL EXECUTIVE COMMITTEE ON GENERAL MOBILIZATION OF THE WORKERS AND POOREST PEASANTS INTO THE WORKERS' AND PEASANTS' RED ARMY[47]

May 29, 1918

The Central Executive Committee considers that the advance from a volunteer army to general mobilization of the workers and poorest peasants is imperatively dictated by the general situation in the country, in order to fight for bread and to repulse the counter-revolution, both domestic and external, whose brazenness has grown in conditions of the famine.

It is necessary to go over without delay to compulsory recruitment of one or several age groups. In view of the complexity of the matter and of the difficulties involved in its simultaneous implementation throughout the country, it appears necessary to begin, on the one hand, with the more threatened areas and, on the other, with the main centres of the workers' movement.

Proceeding from the aforesaid, the Central Executive Committee resolves to instruct the People's Commissariat for Military Affairs to draw up, within a week, a compulsory recruitment plan for Moscow, Petrograd and the Don and Kuban areas, within limits and in forms involving minimum interference in the productive and social life of these areas and cities.

The appropriate Soviet institutions are directed to take the most energetic and active part in the implementation of the tasks with which the Military Commissariat has been charged.

Chairman of the Central Executive Committee, Y. SVERDLOV.
Secretary of the Central Executive Committee, AVANESOV.

Decrees, Vol. 2, pp. 334–335.

58. DECISION OF THE COUNCIL OF PEOPLE'S COMMISSARS ON THE RECOGNITION OF THE GENEVA AND OTHER INTERNATIONAL CONVENTIONS PERTAINING TO THE RED CROSS SOCIETY[48]

May 30, 1918

The Council of People's Commissars of the Russian Soviet Federative Socialist Republic notifies the International Red Cross Committee in Geneva and the governments of all the states which have recognized the Geneva Convention that this convention, both in its original and all later wordings, and all other international conventions and agreements pertaining to the Red Cross, and recognized by Russia prior to October 1917, are recognized and will be observed by the Russian Soviet Government, which retains all the rights and prerogatives stemming from these conventions and agreements.

In view of the fact that certain changes have taken place in the internal organization of the Russian Red Cross Society, about which the International Red Cross Committee will be informed in greater detail later on, the Russian Government deems it necessary to notify the International Red Cross Committee and the Governments of the states which have recognized the Geneva Convention, that all the existing Russian Red Cross organizations are headed by the Russian Red Cross Reorganization Committee, with headquarters in Moscow (3 Armyansky Pereulok).

The Committee has been charged by the Russian Government with the exercise of all functions pertaining to the Red Cross and discharging all rights and prerogatives stemming from the Geneva Convention and other international agreements.

At the present time, after the conclusion of peace, the primary task of the Russian Red Cross is to render assistance to prisoners of war, both Russians in Germany, Austria-Hungary and Turkey, and Germans, Austro-Hungarians and Turks in Russia. In view of this the Russian Government has instructed the Russian Red Cross Society to devote all the energy and all the means at its disposal to the matter of assisting prisoners of war.

The Moscow Prisoner-of-War Relief Committee (302 Sredniye Torgoviye Ryady, Red Square), which is incorporated in the Russian Red Cross Society and whose work of assisting Russian prisoners of war abroad has never been interrupted, retains all rights and privileges which Red Cross agencies enjoy under international conventions and special agreements, and continues to perform all functions it has hitherto been performing. It has been specially instructed by the Russian Government and the Russian Red Cross Committee to devote all its energy to assisting Russian prisoners of war abroad, in which it has been granted a most extensive autonomy. In view of this the Russian Government and the Russian Red Cross Society request the Geneva International Committee, the governments of the countries which have recognized the Geneva Convention, and all the existing Red Cross societies, to co-operate with it in every possible way.

Lastly, the Russian Government, being convinced of the exceptional importance of the problem of prisoners of war, has concentrated all governmental functions pertaining to prisoners of war, civil prisoners and refugees in a special agency, the Central Board for Prisoners of War and Refugees, now stationed at 43 B.Nikitskaya, Moscow, of which it deems necessary to notify the governments and organizations concerned.

Chairman of the Council of People's Commissars, VL. ULYANOV (LENIN).
Commissar for Foreign Affairs, CHICHERIN.
Business Manager of the Council of People's Commissars, VLAD. BONCH-BRUYEVICH.
Secretary of the Council, N. GORBUNOV.

Decrees, Vol. 2, pp. 355–357.

59. DECREE OF THE COUNCIL OF PEOPLE'S COMMISSARS ON THE UNIFICATION OF ALL EDUCATIONAL ESTABLISHMENTS AND INSTITUTIONS UNDER THE PEOPLE'S COMMISSARIAT FOR PUBLIC EDUCATION

May 30, 1918

1. In order to reorganize, unify and renovate education on the principles of new pedagogy and Socialism, all primary, secondary, higher, boarding and ordinary, general and special educational establishments (with the exception of special educational establishments for adults designed for exclusively technical purposes), as well as pre-school and extra-mural educational establishments, whether stateowned, publicly-run or private, are placed under the People's Commissariat for Public Education.

2. All state funds allocated now according to the budgets and establishments of different departments for the needs of public education shall be transferred to the budget of the People's Commissariat for Public Education; simultaneously all properties, buildings with equipment, outbuildings, the land under buildings, fields, manor houses, libraries, teaching aids, valuables, capital, securities and everything else intended for the schools and institutions as designated in Paragraph 1 are handed over to the People's Commissariat for Public Education.

3. The People's Commissariat for Public Education is directed to establish special commissions of its own representatives and those of the departments concerned to determine the dates and order of the transfer indicated in Paragraph 1, which is to be completed before July 15.

Chairman of the Council of People's Commissars, V. ULYANOV (LENIN).
Business Manager of the Council of People's Commissars, VLAD. BONCH-BRUYEVICH.
Secretary of the Council, N. P. GORBUNOV.

Decrees, Vol. 2, pp. 358–359.

60. DECREE OF THE COUNCIL OF PEOPLE'S COMMISSARS ON THE ABOLITION OF DIPLOMATIC RANKS

June 1, 1918

The Russian Socialist Federative Soviet Republic proceeds in its international relations from the recognition of complete equality of nations, big and small.

In virtue of this, revoking paragraphs 826 and 827 of the Institution of Ministries (Code of Laws, Vol. I, Part II, Book 5), the Council of People's Commissars resolves:

1. To abolish the ranks of ambassadors, envoys and other diplomatic representatives, and to designate all representatives of the Russian State accredited to foreign states as plenipotentiary representatives of the Russian Socialist Federative Soviet Republic.

2. In conformity with the fundamental idea of international law, that of intercourse between equal states, to regard all diplomatic agents of foreign states accredited to the Russian Socialist Federative Soviet Republic, irrespective of their rank, as equally plenipotentiary representatives.

Chairman of the Council of the People's Commissars, V. ULYANOV (LENIN).
People's Commissar for Foreign Affairs, CHICHERIN.
Business Manager of the Council of People's Commissars, BONCH-BRUYEVICH.
Secretary of the Council, N. GORBUNOV.

Decrees, Vol. 2, pp. 382–383.

61. PROVISIONAL REGULATIONS OF THE COUNCIL OF PEOPLE'S COMMISSARS ON ANNUAL HOLIDAYS [49]

June 14, 1918

1. Workers and office employees in all sectors of the economy who have worked at an enterprise, in an office or for a private individual for not less than six months without interruption, are entitled to an annual paid holiday, with pay issued in advance.

NOTE. Work at a different enterprise of the same employer or in other institutions of the Russian Federative Soviet Republic, given its continuity, is reckoned in the six-month period.

2. A fortnight's holiday is established for the current year 1918.

3. Utilization of an annual holiday is to be registered in the pay-book or, where this does not exist, in the service record or other appropriate document.

4. Gainful employment during the holiday is forbidden.

5. Holidays are taken throughout the year, their schedule being agreed upon between the employer, the management of the enterprise or office, and representatives of the employees, in such a way that the normal operation of the enterprises or office is not disrupted.

6. Unused holidays are not paid for.

7. Emergency leave of absence is granted in accordance with the procedure indicated in Paragraph 5.

8. The present Regulations do not apply to holidays paid from sickness funds.

9. In 1918, in view of the particular difficulties being experienced by the country, the provisions of all private or collective agreements, and all decisions of local Soviet authorities or separate departments, establishing holidays of longer duration, are cancelled.

10. The People's Commissariat for Labour is given the right to establish longer periods of holiday for persons employed on particularly harmful jobs.

11. These Regulations come into force from the day of publication.

Chairman of the Council of People's Commissars, V. ULYANOV (LENIN).
Business Manager of the Council of People's Commissars, VL. BONCH-BRUYEVICH.
Secretary of the Council, N. GORBUNOV.

Decrees, Vol. 2, pp. 433–434.

62. INSTRUCTIONS OF THE COUNCIL OF PEOPLE'S COMMISSARS ON THE PROCEDURE FOR ENDORSEMENT OF COLLECTIVE AGREEMENTS ON WAGE RATES AND WORKING CONDITIONS

June 25, 1918

1. The present Instructions apply to all collective agreements pertaining to all forms of labour remuneration (daily, piece rate, monthly, by the task, bonuses, fees, etc.) and working conditions, concluded between the trade unions of factory and office workers, on the one side, and employers' unions, companies (commercial or industrial), and state-owned and publicly run enterprises and institutions, on the other.

2. The following should be indicated in the collective agreement:

(*a*) The names and addresses of the trade unions of factory and office workers and those of the public employers concerned;

(*b*) The date of the agreement's entry into force, which cannot come before the presentation of the agreement by the union to the employers;

(*c*) Agencies charged with carrying the agreement into effect, supervising its fulfilment and settling conflicts, as well as measures designed to implement the aforesaid agreement;

(*d*) The procedure for employment and dismissal;

(*e*) Regulations regarding working time (duration of the working day, duration of the lunch break; days off, overtime, annual holidays, etc.);

(*f*) Remuneration: guidelines for fixing payment depending on qualification, the type of work, the degree of complexity and the hazards involved; the procedure for fixing and changing wage rates; the qualification of workers according to trades, and further according to groups and categories; wage rates;

(*g*) Production quotas; the procedure for determining guarantees for the performance of a definite amount of work of a definite quality; the number of persons necessary for performing a definite amount of work;

(*h*) The formation of a body which determines the method of work (wage-rate or technical commissions, etc.).

(*i*) Regulations for the use of flats, canteens, working clothes, etc.;

(*j*) Provisions regarding apprenticeship (age, duration of apprenticeship, instruction, number of apprentices, duration of the working day, remuneration);

(*k*) The period of validity of the agreement; the terms and procedure for amending or terminating it.

3. The draft of the collective agreement, drawn up in accordance with Paragraph 2, is presented by the trade union of the employees to the respective employers' union or society or, in the absence of such, directly to the employers of the given area.

Within seven days after receipt of the copy of the draft the employers must give their reply, stating:

(1) Their acceptance or rejection of the agreement;

(2) Their desire to enter upon negotiations.

4. If the employers' reply is favourable and the sides reach accord, three copies of the draft agreement are submitted for registration, examination, endorsement and validation to: (*a*) the *gubernia* commissar of labour, if the sphere of operation of the agreement lies within the confines of the given *gubernia*; (*b*) the People's Commissariat for Labour, if it is to be effective for the whole of Russia or covers an area greater than one *gubernia*.

NOTE. In Moscow and Petrograd the agreement is submitted to the city commissars for labour.

5. When collective agreements are submitted for endorsement to the People's Commissariat for Labour and its local agencies, the agreements must be accompained by the opinion of the local trade union association or the All-Russian Council of Trade Unions.

6. If the employers' reply is unfavourable, or no accord has been reached during negotiations, the trade union submits the draft agreement, in the manner indicated by Paragraph 4, points "a" and "b", and Paragraph 5, to the commissariats for labour, which decide whether to endorse, modify or reject it.

7. Sessions of the commissariats for labour devoted to the discussion of collective agreements can be attended by representatives of the sides, who provide explanations and data substantiating their demands.

8. Decisions of local commissariats of labour can be appealed against by the parties concerned, within two weeks, to the People's Commissar for Labour.

9. All wage-scale, collective, etc. agreements, standards and rates become effective on the day of their endorsement by the People's Commissariat for Labour or its authorized agencies.

10. If a collective agreement concerns enterprises which are the property of the Russian Socialist Federative Soviet Republic, it is examined by authorized representatives of institutions or managements, with the participation of representatives of the economic council of the district and of the State Control and commissariat for labour of the locality.

Within seven days after its presentation the draft of the said agreement is to be examined and, in keeping with Paragraphs 5–9 of the present Decree, forwarded together with the opinion of the representatives mentioned above for endorsement to the People's Commissariat for Labour.

11. Collective agreements are amended and supplemented by the same procedure by which they are endorsed.

Chairman of the Council of People's Commissars, V. ULYANOV (LENIN).
Deputy People's Commissar for Labour, V. NOGIN.
Business Manager of the Council of People's Commissars, V. BONCH-BRUYEVICH.
Secretary, N. GORBUNOV.

Decrees, Vol. 2, pp. 480–482.

63. DECREE OF THE COUNCIL OF PEOPLE'S COMMISSARS ON THE NATIONALIZATION OF ENTERPRISES IN A NUMBER OF INDUSTRIES, RAILWAY TRANSPORT ENTERPRISES, PUBLIC UTILITIES, AND STEAM MILLS[50]

June 28, 1918

In order to overcome economic dislocation and food shortages, and to consolidate the dictatorship of the working class and the village poor, the Council of People's Commissars has resolved:

I. To declare the following industrial and commercial-industrial enterprises situated on the territory of the Soviet Republic, with all their capital and properties in whatever form, the property of the Russian Socialist Federative Soviet Republic:

In the mining industry

(1) all enterprises owned by joint-stock companies or partnerships, extracting mineral fuel (coal, lignite, combustible shales, anthracite, etc.).

(2) All iron and copper ore mining enterprises owned by joint-stock companies or partnerships.

(3) All platinum mining enterprises.

(4) All tungsten mining enterprises.

(5) All silver, lead and zinc mining enterprises.

(6) All enterprises in the asbestos industry.

(7) The following gold-mining enterprises:

(*a*) the Lena Goldfields Partnership; (*b*) the Kochkar Goldfields Company and all enterprises of the Kochkar system; (*c*) the Upper Amur Gold-Mining Company; (*d*) the Amur Gold-Mining Company; (*e*) the Russian Gold-Mining Company; (*f*) the Fedorovskoye Gold-Mining Company; (*g*) the South Siberian Gold-Mining Company; (*h*) the Amgun-Gold-Mining Company; (*i*) the Miassy Gold-Mining Partnership; (*j*) the South Altai Gold-Mining Company; (*k*) the Olkhovsky Gold Mines Joint-Stock Company; (*l*) the Altai Gold-Mining Company; (*m*) the Lower Selenga Partnership; (*n*) the Tsimanskaye Gold-Mining Company; (*o*) the Mariinsk Goldfields

Company; (*p*) the Yeltsov and Levashov Partnership; (*r*) the Draga Joint-Stock Company; (*s*) the Okhotskoye Gold-Mining Partnership; (*t*) the Aidyrly-Kvarken Goldfields; (*u*) the Moscow Timber Partnership (the North Zaozerye Woodland); (*v*) the Trans-Urals Mining Partnership.

(8) The following salt-extracting enterprises:

(*a*) the Kuli Salt Extracting Company (Lake Kuli); (*b*) the Molla-Kara salt extracting enterprise belonging to Ter-Avanesov; (*c*) all the Usolye salt works;

In the metallurgical and metalworking industries

(9) All enterprises owned by joint-stock companies or partnerships, with a basic capital of one million roubles or more, as well as all large enterprises the aggregate property of which equals or exceeds one million roubles according to the latest balance sheet, and which are engaged in one or several of the following types of production: smelting of iron and copper; manufacturing of semifinished products from them and treatment of the said semi-finished products by rolling, drawing, stamping and by chemical methods; manufacture of all kinds of machines (engines, mechanical implements, agricultural machinery, etc.), aircraft, self-propelled vehicles; shipbuilding, steam locomotives and railway coachbuilding; building of bridges and steel structures; making of precision instruments, firearms, machine-guns, artillery pieces and their parts; manufacture of metal frames and other articles from metal, excluding air brakes.

(10) In addition, all enterprises turning out metal articles which are not manufactured anywhere else in the Russian Federative Republic are declared the property of the Russian Federative Republic, irrespective of the size of their basic capital.

In the textile industry

(11) All cotton-processing enterprises owned by joint-stock companies and partnerships, with a basic capital of not less than one million roubles.

(12) All enterprises owned by joint-stock companies and partnerships which process wool, flax, silk and jute, as well as finishing and dyeing enterprises, with a basic capital of not less than 500,000 roubles.

(13) All hemp-processing enterprises owned by joint stock companies and partnerships, with a basic capital of not less than 200,000 roubles.

In the electrical engineering industry

(14) All power stations owned by joint-stock companies and partnerships, producing electricity for commercial purposes and possessing a basic capital of not less than one million roubles.

(15) All electrical engineering enterprises owned by joint-stock companies and partnerships, manufacturing dynamo machines, electric motors, transformers, electrical measuring instruments and other electrical goods, with a basic capital of not less than one million roubles.

(16) All cable works owned by joint-stock companies and partnerships with a basic capital of not less than one million roubles.

In the timber and woodworking industry

(17) All sawmills owned by joint-stock companies and partnerships, with a basic capital of not less than one million roubles.

(18) All mechanized woodworking enterprises owned by joint-stock companies and partnerships.

In the tobacco industry

(19) All enterprises, owned by joint-stock companies and partnerships, incorporating tobacco factories and having a basic capital of not less than 500,000 roubles (according to 1914 data), and those incorporating shag factories and having a basic capital of not less than 300,000 roubles (according to 1914 data).

In the rubber industry

(20) All enterprises of the rubber industry.

In the glass and ceramic industry

(21) All enterprises owned by joint-stock companies and partnerships, producing glass, cut glass, mirrors, chemical glass, bottle glass, chinaware, faience, pottery, glazed tile, ceramics, majolica and terracotta, with a basic capital of not less than 500,000 roubles (according to 1914 data).

In the leather and shoemaking industry

(22) All shoe-making factories and tanneries owned by joint-stock companies and partnerships with a basic capital of not less than 500,000 roubles (according to 1914 data).

In the cement industry

(23) All cement plant owned by joint-stock companies and partnerships, with a productive capacity of not less than 500,000 barrels a year.

Steam mills

(24) All steam mills owned by joint-stock companies and partnerships, with a fixed capital of not less than 500,000 roubles.

Public utilities

(25) All water-supply enterprises, gas works, electric and horse-driven tramlines and sewerage enterprises throughout the Soviet Republic become the property of the Soviets of Workers' and Peasants' Deputies.

Railway transport

(26) All enterprises of private railway companies, including auxiliary tracks, both in operation and under construction.

In other industries

(27) All cellulose and wood pulp enterprises owned by joint-stock companies and partnerships.

(28) All enterprises of joint-stock companies and partnerships incorporating factories producing writing paper, cardboard, cardboard articles and cigarette paper with basic capital of not less than 300,000 roubles (according to 1914 data).

(29) All enterprises of joint-stock companies and partnerships incorporating artificial fat, soap and stearin works with a basic capital of not less than one million roubles (according to 1914 data), and tallow-melting and oil mills with a basic capital of not less than 500,000 roubles (according to 1914 data).

(30) All enterprises of joint-stock companies and partnerships which incorporate plants producing: (1) mineral acids; (2) calcium, carbide, and (3) charcoal, with a basic capital of not less than 500,000 roubles (according to 1914 data).

(31) All enterprises of the Petrograd Bone-Roasting Company.

(32) Enterprises of: (1) the Joint-Stock Company for the manufacture and marketing of gunpowder (Winner's); (2) the Russian Company for the manufacture and marketing of gunpowder (Schlüsselburg); and (3) the Baranovsky Gunpowder Works Company.

NOTE. Unless specified otherwise, the basic capital of joint-stock companies and partnerships is calculated according to data for 1916 or the last period accounted for ending in 1916. In the case of enterprises founded after 1916 the calculation is carried out according to the latest data for the year when the statute of the enterprise was approved.

II. The appropriate departments of the Supreme Economic Council are instructed urgently to organize management of the nationalized enterprises, with observance of all the previously issued relevant decrees and under the general guidance of the presidium of the Supreme Economic Council.

With respect to the enterprises mentioned in Section I, Paragraph 24 of this Decree (steam mills), this commission is entrusted to the Commissariat for Food Supply with full observance of all the previously issued decrees on the management of nationalized enterprises.

With respect to the enterprises mentioned in Section I, Paragraph 25 of this Decree (public utilities), the same commission is entrusted, on the same condition, to the local Soviets of Workers' and Peasants' Deputies.

With respect to the enterprises mentioned in Section I, Paragraph 26 of this Decree (railways and subsidiary lines), the same commission is entrusted to the Commissariat of Railways, subject to ultimate approval by the Council of People's Commissars.

III. Pending a special decision of the Supreme Economic Council regarding each particular enterprise, the enterprises declared under this Decree to be the property of the Russian Soviet Federative Socialist Republic are regarded as leased to their former owners gratis; their boards and former owners continue to finance them and receive profits in the usual manner.

IV. From the moment of the issue of this Decree, the board members, directors and other executives of nationalized enterprises are accountable to the Soviet Republic for their safety and normal operation.

Those who abandon their offices without the consent of the appropriate agencies of the supreme Economic Council, or inexcusably mismanage the affairs of the enterprise, not only answer to the Republic with all their property but will be prosecuted in the courts of the Republic as for a grave criminal offence.

V. The entire office, technical and operative personnel of a nationalized enterprise, as well as the directors, board members and other executives, are declared to be in the service of the Soviet Socialist Federative Republic, and are paid according to the rates that existed prior to nationalization, out of the profits and working capital of the enterprise.

Members of the technical and managerial personnel of nationalized enterprises who abandon their offices are answerable to a revolutionary tribunal, with all the severity of the law.

VI. The personal means of board members, shareholders and owners of nationalized enterprises are sequestered until the relationship of the sums involved to the working capital and resources of the enterprises is ascertained.

VII. The boards of all nationalized enterprises are instructed to draw up without delay balance-sheets as on July 1, 1918.

VIII. The Supreme Economic Council is instructed to work out in the shortest time possible, and to dispatch to all nationalized enterprises, detailed instructions on the organization of management and on the tasks of the workers' organizations stemming from this decree.

IX. Enterprises belonging to consumers' cooperative societies and partnerships and their associations are not subject to conversion into the property of the Republic.

X. This Decree becomes effective from the day of its signing.
Moscow, June 28, 1918.

Chairman of the Council of People's Commissars, V. ULYANOV (LENIN).
People's Commissars: TSYURUPA, NOGIN.
Business Manager of the Council of People's Commissars, V. BONCH-BRUYEVICH.
Secretary of the Council, N. GORBUNOV.

Decrees, Vol. 2, pp. 498–503.

64. CONSTITUTION (FUNDAMENTAL LAW) OF THE R.S.F.S.R. ADOPTED BY THE FIFTH ALL-RUSSIA CONGRESS OF SOVIETS[51]

DECISION OF THE FIFTH ALL-RUSSIA CONGRESS OF SOVIETS, ADOPTED ON JULY 10, 1918

The Declaration of Rights of the Working and Exploited People, approved by the Third All-Russia Congress of Soviets in January 1918, together with the Constitution of the Soviet Republic approved by the Fifth Congress, make up the single fundamental law of the Russian Socialist Federative Soviet Republic.

This fundamental law becomes effective from the moment of its publication in final form in *Izvestia Vserossiiskogo Tsentralnogo Ispolnitelnogo Komiteta*. It shall be published by all local organs of Soviet government and prominently displayed in all Soviet institutions.

The Fifth Congress instructs the People's Commissariat for Public Education to introduce in all schools and other educational establishments of the Russian Republic, without exception, the study of the basic provisions of the present Constitution, as well as their explanation and interpretation.

Part One

DECLARATION OF RIGHTS OF THE WORKING AND EXPLOITED PEOPLE*

Part Two

GENERAL PROVISIONS OF THE CONSTITUTION OF THE R.S.F.S.R.

9. The main objective of the Constitution of the Russian Socialist Federative Soviet Republic, designed for the present transitional period, is to establish the dictatorship of the urban and rural proletariat and the poorest peasantry in the form of a powerful All-Russia Soviet Government, with a view to completely suppressing the bourgeoisie, abolishing exploitation

* Since the Declaration was published earlier in this book, its text is not repeated here (see No. 29).

of man by man, and establishing Socialism, under which there will be neither division into classes nor state power.

10. The Russian Republic is a free socialist society of all the working people of Russia. All power in the Russian Socialist Federative Soviet Republic belongs to the entire working population of the country united in urban and rural Soviets.

11. The Soviets of regions with a distinct mode of living and national composition can unite in autonomous regional unions at the head of which, as at the head of all regional unions that can be eventually formed, stand regional congresses of Soviets and their executive agencies.

These autonomous regional unions form, on a federal basis, component parts of the Russian Socialist Federative Soviet Republic.

12. Supreme power in the Russian Socialist Federative Soviet Republic is exercised by the All-Russia Congress of Soviets, and in the intervals between Congresses by the All-Russia Central Executive Committee.

13. In order to ensure genuine freedom of conscience for the working people, the church is separated from the State, and the school from the church: and freedom of religious and anti-religious propaganda is recognized for all citizens.

14. In order to ensure genuine freedom of expression for the working people, the Russian Socialist Federative Soviet Republic abolishes the dependence of the press on capital, and places at the disposal of the working class and the poor peasantry all the technical and material requisites for the publication of newspaper, pamphlets, books and all other printed matter, and guarantees their unhindered circulation throughout the country.

15. In order to ensure genuine freedom of assembly for the working people, the Russian Socialist Federative Soviet Republic, recognizing the right of citizens of the Soviet Republic freely to hold assemblies, meetings, processions, etc. places at the disposal of the working class and the poor peasantry all buildings suitable for the holding of public gatherings, complete with furnishing, lighting and heating.

16. In order to ensure genuine freedom of association for the working people, the Russian Socialist Federative Soviet Republic, having destroyed the economic and political rule of

the propertied classes and thereby removed all the obstacles which heretofore, in bourgeois society, prevented the workers and peasants from enjoying freedom of organization and action, renders material and all other assistance to the workers and poorest peasants for purposes of their association and organization.

17. In order to ensure access to knowledge for the working people, the Russian Socialist Federative Soviet Republic makes its aim to give the workers and poorest peasants complete all-round and free education.

18. The Russian Socialist Federative Soviet Republic declares labour to be the duty of all citizens of the Republic, and proclaims the slogan: "He who does not work, neither shall he eat!"

19. In order to safeguard the gains of the great workers' and peasants' revolution, the Russian Socialist Federative Republic declares defence of the socialist Fatherland to be the duty of all the citizens of the Republic and introduces universal military service. The honourable right of bearing arms in defence of the revolution is granted only to working people; non-working elements are enlisted for other military duties.

20. Proceeding from the principle of solidarity of the working people of all nations, the Russian Socialist Federative Soviet Republic grants full political rights of Russian citizens to foreigners residing in the territory of the Russian Republic for purposes of employment, and belonging to the working class or to the peasantry not employing the labour of others: and it empowers the local Soviets to grant to such foreigners, without any cumbersome formalities, Russian citizenship rights.

21. The Russian Socialist Federative Soviet Republic grants the right of asylum to all foreigners subjected to persecution for political and religious crimes.

22. The Russian Socialist Federative Soviet Republic, recognizing the equality of rights of all citizens, irrespective of their race or nationality, declares the establishment or toleration on this basis of any privileges or advantages, or any oppression of national minorities or restriction of their equality, to be contraventions of the fundamental laws of the Republic.

23. Guided by the interests of the working class as a whole, the Russian Socialist Federative Soviet Republic deprives

individuals and groups of rights which they utilize to the detriment of the socialist revolution.

Part Three

THE STRUCTURE OF SOVIET GOVERNMENT

A. Organization of the central authority

Chapter Six

THE ALL-RUSSIA CONGRESS OF SOVIETS OF WORKERS', PEASANTS', COSSACKS' AND RED ARMY MEN'S DEPUTIES

24. The All-Russia Congress of Soviets is the supreme authority of the Russian Socialist Federative Soviet Republic.

25. The All-Russia Congress of Soviets is composed of representatives of urban Soviets on the basis of one deputy for every 25,000 electors, and representatives of *gubernia* congresses of Soviets on the basis of one deputy for every 125,000 of the population.

NOTE 1. In the event of a *gubernia* congress of Soviets not preceding the All-Russia Congress, delegates to the latter are sent directly by *uyezd* congresses.

NOTE 2. In the event of a regional congress of Soviets directly preceding the All-Russia Congress, delegates to the latter can be sent by the regional congress.

26. The All-Russia Congress of Soviets is convened by the All-Russia Central Executive Committee at least twice a year.

27. An extraordinary All-Russia Congress of Soviets is convened by the All-Russia Central Executive Committee on its own initiative, or on the demand of the Soviets of localities inhabited by at least one-third of the population of the Republic.

28. The All-Russia Congress of Soviets elects the All-Russia Central Executive Committee, to consist of not more than 200 members.

29. The All-Russia Central Executive Committee is fully accountable to the All-Russia Congress of Soviets.

30. In the intervals between Congresses the All-Russia Central Executive Committee is the supreme authority of the Republic.

Chapter Seven

THE ALL-RUSSIA CENTRAL EXECUTIVE COMMITTEE

31. The All-Russia Central Executive Committee is the highest legislative, administrative and supervisory body of the Russian Socialist Federative Soviet Republic.

32. The All-Russia Central Executive Committee gives general directives for the activity of the Workers' and Peasants' Government and all organs of Soviet power in the country; unites and coordinates legislative and administrative activities, and supervises the implementation of the Soviet Constitution and of the decisions of All-Russia Congresses of Soviets and the central bodies of Soviet power.

33. The All-Russia Central Executive Committee examines and approves draft decrees and other proposals submitted by the Council of People's Commissars or by separate departments, and issues its own decrees and ordinances.

34. The All-Russia Central Executive Committee convenes the All-Russia Congress of Soviets, to which it submits an account of its activity and reports on general policy and particular matters.

35. The All-Russian Central Executive Committee appoints the Council of People's Commissars for general management of the affairs of the Russian Socialist Federative Soviet Republic, and departments (People's Commissariats) to be in charge of particular branches of the administration.

36. The members of the All-Russia Central Executive Committee work in the departments (People's Commissariats) or carry out special commissions of the All-Russia Central Executive Committee.

Chapter Eight

THE COUNCIL OF PEOPLE'S COMMISSARS

37. The Council of People's Commissars exercises general management of the affairs of the Russian Socialist Federative Soviet Republic.

38. In pursuance of this task the Council of People's Commissars issues decrees, ordinances, instructions and generally

takes what measures are necessary to ensure the proper course of life of the State.

39. The Council of People's Commissars immediately notifies the All-Russia Central Executive Committee of all its orders and decisions.

40. The All-Russia Central Executive Committee has the right to cancel or suspend any order or decision of the Council of People's Commissars.

41. All decisions and orders of the Council of People's Commissars which are of major general political importance are submitted to the All-Russia Central Executive Committee for consideration and approval.

NOTE. Urgent measures can be taken by the Council of People's Commissars directly.

42. Members of the Council of People's Commissars head the People's Commissariats.

43. Eighteen People's Commissariats are formed: (*a*) Foreign Affairs; (*b*) Military Affairs; (*c*) Maritime Affairs; (*d*) Interior; (*e*) Justice; (*f*) Labour; (*g*) Social Security; (*h*) Public Education; (*i*) Post and Telegraph; (*j*) Nationalities Affairs; (*k*) Finance; (*l*) Transport; (*m*) Agriculture; (*n*) Trade and Industry; (*o*) Food Supply; (*p*) State Control; (*q*) the Supreme Economic Council; (*r*) Public Health.

44. Under the chairmanship of every People's Commissar a board is constituted whose members are confirmed by the Council of People's Commissars.

45. The People's Commissar has the right personally to take decisions on all matters that come within the competence of his Commissariat. In the event of its disagreement with a decision of the People's Commissar the board can, without suspending the implementation of the decision, appeal against it to the Council of People's Commissars or the Presidium of the All-Russia Central Executive Committee.

The same right of appeal belongs to individual members of the board.

46. The Council of People's Commissars is fully accountable to the All-Russia Congress of Soviets and the All-Russia Central Executive Committee.

47. The People's Commissars and the boards of the People's Commissariats are fully accountable to the Council of People's

Commissars and the All-Russia Central Executive Committee.

48. The rank of People's Commissar is given exclusively to members of the Council of People's Commissars, which manages the general affairs of the Russian Socialist Federative Soviet Republic, and cannot be conferred on any other representative of Soviet government either in the centre or in the provinces.

Chapter Nine

THE JURISDICTION OF THE ALL-RUSSIA CONGRESS OF SOVIETS AND THE ALL-RUSSIA CENTRAL EXECUTIVE COMMITTEE

49. Within the jurisdiction of the All-Russia Congress of Soviets and the Central Executive Committee come all matters of State importance, viz:

(*a*) Approval and amendment of the Constitution of the Russian Socialist Federative Soviet Republic.

(*b*) General guidance of the foreign and domestic policy of the Russian Socialist Federative Soviet Republic.

(*c*) Delimitation and modification of frontiers, as well as alienation of parts of the territory of the Russian Socialist Federative Soviet Republic or of rights belonging to it.

(*d*) Delimitation of the boundaries and spheres of jurisdiction of the regional unions of Soviets forming part of the Russian Socialist Federative Soviet Republic, as well as settlement of disputes between them.

(*e*) Admission of new members into the Russian Socialist Federative Soviet Republic and confirmation of secession of parts of the Russian Federation.

(*f*) General determination of the administrative divisions of the territory of the Russian Socialist Federative Soviet Republic, and confirmation of regional formations.

(*g*) Establishment and modification of the system of weights and measures and the monetary system on the territory of the Russian Socialist Federative Soviet Republic.

(*h*) Relations with foreign States, declaration of war and conclusion of peace.

(*i*) Contracting and granting of loans, conclusion of customs and trade treaties and financial agreements.

(*j*) Determination of the fundamentals and the general plan of the national economy and its branches on the territory of the Russian Socialist Federative Soviet Republic.

(*k*) Approval of the budget of the Russian Socialist Federative Soviet Republic.

(*l*) Establishment of federal taxes and duties.

(*m*) Definition of the basic principles of organization of the armed forces of the Russian Socialist Federative Soviet Republic.

(*n*) Federal legislation, the judicial system and judicial procedure, civil and criminal legislation, etc.

(*o*) Appointment and dismissal of individual members of the Council of People's Commissars and of the Council of People's Commissars as a whole, as well as confirmation of the Chairman of the Council of People's Commissars.

(*p*) General regulations on the acquisition and loss of Russian citizenship rights and on the rights of foreigners on the territory of the Republic.

(*q*) The right of amnesty, general and partial.

50. In addition to the matters listed above, the All-Russian Congress of Soviets and the All-Russia Central Executive Committee decide all questions which they find coming within their competence.

51. It is the exclusive prerogative of the All-Russian Congress of Soviets to:

(*a*) define and amend the basic principles of the Soviet Constitution;

(*b*) ratify peace treaties.

52. The All-Russia Central Executive Committee may decide matters indicated in paragraphs (*c*) and (*h*) of Article 49 only when an All-Russian Congress of Soviets cannot be convened.

B. Organization of Local Soviet Authority

Chapter Ten

CONGRESSES OF SOVIETS

53. Congresses of Soviets are composed as follows:

(*a*) Regional (*oblast*) congresses—of representatives of city Soviets and *uyezd* congresses, on the basis of one delegate per 25,000 residents, and from cities, one delegate per 5,000 electors, with not more than 500 delegates from the region as a whole; or of representatives of *gubernia* congresses of Soviets, elected on the same basis, if such congresses directly precede the regional congress.

(*b*) *Gurbernia* area congresses—of representatives of city Soviets and *volost* congresses, on the basis of one delegate per 10,000 residents and from cities, one deputy per 2,000 electors, with not more than 300 delegates from the *gubernia* (area) as a whole. If *uyezd* congresses of Soviets directly precede the *gubernia* congress, elections are conducted on the same basis, by *uyezd* rather than *volost* congresses.

(*c*) *Uyezd* (district) congresses—of representatives of village Soviets, on the basis of one delegate per 1,000 residents, with not more than 300 delegates from the *uyezd* (district) as a whole.

(*d*) *Volost* congresses—of representatives of all village Soviets of the *volost*, on the basis of one delegate for every ten members of a Soviet.

NOTE 1. *Uyezd* congresses are attended by representatives of the Soviets of towns whose population does not exceed 10,000; village Soviets of localities with a population of less than 1,000 unite to elect delegates to the *uyezd* congress.

NOTE 2. Village Soviets having less than ten members send to the *volost* congress one representative each.

54. Congresses of Soviets are convened by the respective local executive bodies of Soviet authority (executive committees) at their discretion, or on the demand of the Soviets of localities accounting for not less than one-third of the population of the given territorial unit: but in any event at least twice a year in a region, once in every three months in a *gubernia* or *uyezd*, and once a month in a *volost*.

55. The region, *gubernia*, *uyezd* or *volost* congress of Soviets elects its executive committee, to consist of not more than: (*a*) 25 members in a region or *gubernia*; (*b*) 20 in an *uyezd*, and (*c*) 10 in a *volost*. The executive committee is fully accountable to the congress of Soviets that elected it.

56. Within the boundaries of its region, *gubernia*, *uyezd* or *volost*, the congress of Soviets is the highest authority; in the intervals between congresses this authority is vested in the executive committee.

Chapter Eleven
SOVIETS OF DEPUTIES

57. The Soviets of deputies are composed as follows:

(*a*) In cities—on the basis of one deputy per 1,000 of the population, but with not less than 50 and not more than 1,000 members.

(*b*) In rural localities (villages, Cossack-settlements, towns with less than 10,000 residents, auls, hamlets, etc.)—on the basis of one deputy per 100 of the population, but with not less than three and not more than 50 deputies per locality.

The term of office of deputies is three months.

NOTE. In those rural localities where this is recognized as practicable, matters of administration are decided directly by a general meeting of the electors.

58. For day-to-day work, the Soviets of deputies elect, from among their members, executive bodies (executive committees) consisting of not more than 5 members in villages, and on the basis of one member per 50 deputies, but with not less than three and not more than 15 members, in cities (not more than 40 members in Petersburg and Moscow). The executive committee is fully accountable to the Soviet which elected it.

59. Sessions of the Soviet of deputies are convened by the executive committee at its discretion, or on the demand of not less than half of the deputies to the Soviet: but at least once a week in cities and twice a week in rural areas.

60. Within the boundaries of the given locality Soviet or, in the event envisaged in Article 57 (Note), the general meeting of electors, is the highest authority.

Chapter Twelve
THE JURISDICTION OF LOCAL BODIES OF SOVIET RULE

61. The regional, *gubernia*, *uyezd* and *volost* bodies of Soviet rule and the Soviets of deputies:

(*a*) Put into effect all decisions of the corresponding higher bodies of Soviet rule;

(*b*) take all measures to promote the cultural and economic development of the given territory;

(*c*) decide all questions of purely local (for the given territory, importance;

(*d*) coordinate all Soviet activity within the boundaries of the given territory.

62. The congresses of Soviets and their executive bodies have the right of control over the activities of the local Soviets (i.e. those of regions have the right of control over all the Soviets of the given region; those of *gubernias*, over all the Soviets of the given *gubernia*, with the exception of city Soviets not forming parts of *uyezd* congresses, etc.); the regional and *gubernia* congresses and their executive committees have, in addition, the right to cancel decisions of the Soviets functioning in their localities, notifying, in the most important instances, the central Soviet authority.

63. To ensure fulfilment of the tasks developing on the organs of Soviet authority, city and village Soviets and regional, *gubernia*, *uyezd* and *volost* executive committees set up corresponding departments and appoint their heads.

Part Four

ACTIVE AND PASSIVE SUFFRAGE

Chapter Thirteen

64. The right to elect and to be elected to Soviets is enjoyed, irrespective of religion, nationality, sex, domicile, etc. by the following citizens of the Russian Socialist Federative Soviet Republic who have reached the age of eighteen by polling day:

(*a*) All those who earn a living by productive and socially useful labour (as well as persons engaged in housekeeping which enables the former to work productively), viz. wage and salaried workers of all groups and categories engaged in industry, trade, agriculture, etc. and peasants and Cossack farmers who do not employ hired labour for profit;

(*b*) Soldiers of the Soviet army and navy;

(*c*) Citizens belonging to categories listed in Paragraphs (*a*) and (*b*) of the present article who have been to any degree incapacitated.

Note 1. The local Soviets may, subject to approval by the

central authority, lower the age limit established in the present article.

NOTE 2. As far as resident foreigners are concerned, active and passive suffrage is enjoyed by persons indicated in Article 20 (part Two, Chapter V).

65. The right to elect and to be elected is denied to the following persons, even if they belong to one of the categories listed above:

(*a*) Persons who employ hired labour for profit;

(*b*) Persons living on unearned income, such as interest on capital, profits from enterprises, receipts from property, etc.;

(*c*) Private traders and commercial middle-men;

(*d*) Monks and ministers of religion;

(*e*) Employees and agents of the former police, the special corps of gendarmerie and the secret political police department, as well as members of the former imperial family;

(*f*) Persons declared insane by legal proceeding, as well as persons in ward;

(*g*) persons condemned for pecuniary and infamous crimes to terms established by law or by a court decision.

Chapter Fourteen

THE CONDUCT OF ELECTIONS

66. Elections are held, according to established customs, on days appointed by local Soviets.

67. Elections are conducted in the presence of an electoral commission and a representative of the local Soviet.

68. In instances when the presence of a representative of Soviet authority is technically impossible, he is replaced by the electoral commission chairman or, in the absence of the latter, by the chairman of the electoral assembly.

69. The proceedings and results of the election are recorded in a minute signed by the members of the electoral commission and the representative of the Soviet.

70. The detailed procedure for the conduct of elections, and for the participation in them of trade unions and other workers' organizations, is determined by the local Soviets in keeping with instructions issued by the All-Russia Central Executive Committee.

Chapter Fifteen

VERIFICATION AND REVOCATION OF ELECTION RETURNS: RECALL OF DEPUTIES

71. All material pertaining to the conduct of elections is forwarded to the respective Soviet.

72. The Soviet appoints a credentials committee to verify the results of the elections.

73. The credentials committee reports to the Soviet on its findings.

74. The Soviet decides the question of confirming disputed candidates.

75. Should the Soviet reject a candidate, it appoints re-elections.

76. Should the elections as a whole be found faulty, the question of quashing them is decided by the higher body of Soviet rule.

77. The final instance for quashing elections to Soviets is the All-Russia Central Executive Committee.

78. The electors who have sent a deputy to the Soviet have the right to recall him at any time, and to hold new elections, in keeping with the general rules.

Part Five

BUDGETARY LAW

Chapter Sixteen

79. The main objective of the fiscal policy of the Russian Socialist Federative Soviet Republic in the current transitional period of the dictatorship of the working people is expropriation of the bourgeoisie and preparation of conditions for the universal equality of the citizens of the Republic in the sphere of production and distribution of values. It is therefore aimed at placing at the disposal of the organs of Soviet power all the means necessary for satisfying the local and national needs of the Soviet Republic, in the pursuit of which tasks it will not stop at invading the sphere of the right of private ownership.

80. The State revenues and expenditures of the Russian Socialist Federative Soviet Republic are united in the State budget.

81. The All-Russian Congress of Soviets or the All-Russia Central Executive Committee determine which revenues and duties accrue to the State budget and which are placed at the disposal of the local Soviets, and establish the limits of taxation.

82. The Soviets collect taxes and rates for exclusively local economic needs. The requirements of the State as a whole are met out of resources allocated by the State Treasury.

83. No expenditures can be made out of the resources of the State Treasury unless provided for in the State budget, or without a special decision of the central authority.

84. To meet needs of national importance, local Soviets are allotted credits by the appropriate People's Commissariats out of State Treasury funds.

85. All State Treasury credits, and credits approved for local needs, are expanded by Soviets strictly as provided for in their budgets, and cannot be used for other purposes without a special decision of the All-Russian Central Executive Committee and the Council of People's Commissars.

86. Local Soviets draw up half-yearly and yearly estimates of revenues and expenditures for local needs. The estimates of village and *volost* Soviets and Soviets of cities participating in *uyezd* congresses, and those of the *uyezd* organs of Soviet power, are approved by the respective *gubernia* and *oblast* congresses or their executive committees; the estimates of city, *gubernia* and regional bodies of Soviet power are approved by the All-Russia Central Executive Committee and the Council of People's Commissars.

87. Should the need arise for expenditures insufficiently provided for in the estimates, or not provided for at all, the Soviets apply for additional allocations to the respective People's Commissariats.

88. In the event of local resources proving insufficient to satisfy local needs, the issue of subsidies or loans to local Soviets necessary to cover urgent expenditures is authorized by the All-Russia Central Executive Committee and the Council of People's Commissars.

Part Six

THE ARMS AND THE FLAG OF THE RUSSIAN SOCIALIST FEDERATIVE SOVIET REPUBLIC

Chapter Seventeen

89. The Arms of the Russian Socialist Federative Soviet Republic consist of a sickle and a hammer with their handles crossed, pointing downwards, gold upon a red field in the sun's rays, and surrounded by a wreath of ears of grain, with the inscriptions:

(*a*) "Russian Socialist Federative Soviet Republic", and

(*b*) "Proletarians of all Countries, Unite!"

90. The flag and ensign of the Russian Socialist Federative Soviet Republic is of red cloth with the gold letters "RSFSR" or the words "Russian Socialist Federative Soviet Republic" in the left upper corner near the staff.

Chairman of the Fifth All-Russia Congress of Soviets and of the All-Russia Central Executive Committee, Y. SVERDLOV.

Members of the Presidium of the All-Russia Central Executive Committee: G. I. TEODOROVICH, F. A. ROZIN, A. K. MITROFANOV, K. G. MAXIMOV.

Secretary of the All-Russia Central Executive Committee, V. A. AVANESOV.

Decrees, Vol. 2, pp. 550–564.

EXPLANATORY NOTES

1. The Appeal was drafted by Lenin in the flat of V. D. Bonch-Bruyevich, a professional revolutionary later to become the first business manager of the Soviet government. On the same day the document was published in the newspaper *Rabochi i Soldat* (Worker and Soldier) and in leaflet form and widely circulated in Petrograd.

2. The Appeal was drafted by Lenin and adopted at the first sitting of the Second All-Russia Congress of Soviets of Workers' and Soldiers' Deputies.

The Second Congress was held at Smolny Institute in Petrograd on November 7–8 (October 25–26), 1917. The Congress opened at 10.40 p.m. on November 7 (October 25) with 649 delegates present, among them 390 Bolsheviks. After the opening of the Congress the Mensheviks, Right Socialist-Revolutionaries and Bundists, seeing that the majority supported the Bolsheviks, walked out. Shortly after 3.00 a.m., November 8 (October 26), the Congress heard the report of the capture of the Winter Palace and the arrest of members of the bourgeois Provisional Government and adopted the Appeal "To Workers, Soldiers and Peasants!" The first sitting closed after 5.00 a.m.

The second sitting, opening at 9.00 a.m., heard Lenin's reports on peace and on land, and passed the Decrees on Peace (see Document 3), on Land (see Document 4) and on the Formation of the Workers' and Peasants' Government (see Document 5), as drafted by Lenin. It also adopted decisions on the abolition of capital punishment in the army in the field and on the immediate arrest of Kerensky, the appeal "To All Railwaymen!", decisions on the power takeover by the Soviets and on the release of the arrested members of land committees, on the measures to be taken against counter-revolutionary acts and on the formation of temporary revolutionary committees in the army, and the appeal "To Cossack Brothers!" The Congress elected a new All-Russia Central Executive Committee (ARCEC) consisting of 101 members, among them 62 Bolsheviks, 29 Left-Wing Socialist-Revolutionaries, six Internationalist Social-Democrats, three representatives of the Ukrainian Socialist Party, and one Maximalist Socialist-Revolutionary.

3. The Decree on Peace was read out by Lenin at the second sitting of the Second All-Russia Congress of Soviets and was unanimously adopted after 10.00 p.m., November 8 (October 26).

See also Documents 11, 18, 31, 44, 56.

4. The Decree on Land was passed at the second sitting of the Second All-Russia Congress of Soviets at 2.00 a.m., November 9 (October 27), 1917.

In development of the decree, on February 9 (January 27), 1917, the ARCEC and the Council of People's Commissars (CPC) enacted the Basic Law on the Socialization of Land, drafted by the peasant section of the Third All-Russia Congress of Soviets. The Law reaffirmed the general provisions of the Decree on Land, determined the order of land tenure and concretized questions of resettlement, forms of land tenure, the order of acquisition of rights of land tenure, and other matters. Since the Law was drafted with the participation of the Left-Wing Socialist-Revolutionaries, some of its provisions bore traces of a petty-bourgeois understanding of problems of land tenure and land utilization. Therefore, by decision of the First All-Russia Congress of Land Departments, a new law was drawn up. On February 14, 1919, the government newspaper *Izvestia* published the instructions of the ARCEC on socialist land tenure and on measures to ensure transition to farming along socialist lines. The instructions laid down principles of socialist land tenure and of the organization of state farms and agricultural communes, and established labour quotas in collective farming.

5. The Decree was drafted by Lenin and adopted at the close of the second sitting of the Second All-Russia Congress of Soviets.

6. The Decree on the Press was the first law issued by the Council of People's Commissars. On November 17 (4), 1917, the decree was endorsed by the ARCEC, with V. I. Lenin speaking in favour of the said document.

On February 10 (January 28), 1918, in development of the Decree, a Revolutionary Tribunal for the Press was set up to deal with all "crimes and misdeeds against the people committed through the medium of the press," such as "publication of false or biased information about phenomena of social life, inasmuch as such information is prejudicial to the rights and interests of the revolutionary people, as well as violations of ordinances regarding the press issued by the Soviet Government."

7. This Decree was the first step towards the demobilization of the old army. Problems of demobilization were also dealt with at a conference late in November 1917 and at the Army Congress on the Demobilization of the Army, held in December 1917–January 1918.

"There is no army as such, there is no possibility of holding it together. The best thing to do is to demobilize it as soon as possible. It is an afflicted part of the organism. It has been subjected to untold torments and hardships in the war, which it entered technically unprepared and from which it has emerged in a such a state that it panics at every offensive. This cannot be blamed on people who have endured such untold suffering.

"It is a sick part of the Russian state organism which cannot bear the burden of this war any longer. The sooner we demobilize it, the quicker it will dissolve amidst units that are not so seriously afflicted yet, and the sooner the country will get prepared to withstand new grave trials." (Lenin at the 7th Congress of the CPSU, March 1918).

For matters of the reorganization and command of the army see Documents 23 and 24.

8. The Decree was published in the Government newspapers *Izvestia* No. 223. November 25 (12), 1917, and *Gazeta Vremennogo Rabochego i Krestyanskogo Pravitelstva* (Gazette of the Provisional Workers' and Peasants' Government) No. 9, November 25 (12), 1917, and in the central organ of the Bolshevik Party, *Pravda*, evening issue No. 10, November 26 (13), 1917.

9. It was announced in the appeal of the Petrograd Revolutionary Military Committee, "To the Citizens of Russia!", dated November 7 (October 25), 1917, that workers' control over production had become a fact (see Document 1). On subsequent days, before November 13 (October 31), Lenin wrote the draft of the regulations, which was published in a somewhat modified form in *Gazeta Vremennogo Rabochego i Krestyanskogo Pravitelstva* on November 14 (1) and three days later in *Pravda*. Simultaneously the bureau of the Council of Factory Committees prepared its own draft. On November 27 (14) the ARCEC discussed this question and adopted Lenin's version with slight amendments.

10. The Decree was drafted by Lenin and discussed at the ARCEC sitting on December 4 (November 21), 1917. Presenting the Decree, Lenin said, among other things: "The question of recall is one of genuine implementation of the principle of democracy." After debates the decree was referred to the Coordinating Commission and later at 2.00 a.m., unanimously passed at the same sitting of the ARCEC.

11. In development of, and in addition to, the Decree of the Judicature, the ARCEC and the CPC adopted the following laws:

on January 11, 1918 (December 29, 1917)—the decree on the pendent cases of the abolished judicial institutions; on January 22 (9)—the decree on the commissions for minors, under which juveniles were not subject to prosecution; on February 10–January 28—the decree on the Revolutionary Tribunal for the Press; on February 15—Decree No. 2 on Judicature (see Document 41), and on February 16—the decree on the court of arbitration.

On May 4, by way of amending Paragraph 8 of the Decree on Judicature, the CPC passed a decree on revolutionary tribunals, under which revolutionary tribunals were to be preserved only in the capitals (Petrograd and Moscow), *gubernia* cities, at large railway junctions and in industrial centres. These were to combat counter-revolution, sabotage, profiteering, pogroms, corruption, forgery, misuse of Soviet documents, hooliganism and espionage. On May 29 the ARCEC Chairman, Y. M. Sverdlov, and the CPC Chairman, V. I. Lenin, signed the Statute of the Revolutionary Tribunal of the ARCEC, which was to try the most important cases removed from the cognizance of local tribunals by decisions of the Presidium of the ARCEC, the CPC and the People's Commissariat of Justice.

12. During the discussion of the draft of the Decree by the CPC Lenin suggested adding the word "machines" to the words "agricultural implements" in Paragraph 1. On April 24, 1918, in development of this Decree, the CPC adopted a decree establishing a State monopoly of agricultural machines and implements (see Document 53).

13. The Decree was drafted by Lenin and endorsed by the CPC on December 11 (November 28), 1917. The Left-Wing Socialist-Revolutionaries, who participated in the ARCEC, entered a protest against the arrest of the Constitutional-Democrat members of the Constituent Assembly. On December 14 (1) their protest was discussed and rejected by the ARCEC, which laid it down in its decision that it "reaffirms the need for the most resolute struggle against the bourgeois counter-revolution headed by the Constitutional-Democratic Party, which has launched a bitter civil war against the very foundations of the workers' and peasants' revolution", and stressed in conclusion that it "rejects the protests of the political groups whose vacillations undermine the dictatorship of the proletariat and the poor peasantry".

14. The question of establishing a centre to manage the national economy was first posed at a CPC sitting on November 24 (11).

1917. On Lenin's proposal a preparatory commission was set up. On November 28 (15) the draft decree was submitted to the CPC, and on December 1 (November 18) it was adopted and forwarded to the ARCEC, which approved it on December 14 (1).

On August 8, 1918, the CPC approved the statute of the Supreme Economic Council (SEC), under which the SEC constituted as the economic department of the ARCEC accountable to the latter and and to the CPC was to regulate and organize all production and distribution and administer all the enterprises of the country. General guidance of the SEC activity was exercised by a plenum consisting of 69 representatives of the ARCEC, the All-Union Central Council of Trade Unions, the regional economic councils, the workers' cooperatives, and seven People's Commissariats. The day-to-day work of the SEC was directed by a presidium consisting of nine members, eight being elected by the plenum and the ninth, chairman, with the rights of a People's Commissar, appointed by the ARCEC.

15. The draft of the Rules was prepared by the People's Commissariat of Labour. On November 28 (15), 1917, it was discussed at a CPC sitting which decided to publish it and instructed all People's Commissars to familiarize themselves with it and communicate their conclusions to the ARCEC. On December 2 (November 19) the draft was printed in *Pravda*. On December 14 (1) the ARCEC considered the draft and set up a commission to examine it, jointly with the ARCEC Presidium, and submit it for approval to the CPC. On December 24 (11) the Secretary of the ARCEC sent the draft to the newspapers for immediate publication. On December 26 (13) the Rules were approved by the CPC.

See also Document 39.

16. The draft of the decision was prepared by the People's Commissariat of Public Education and submitted by People's Commissar A. V. Lunacharsky to the CPC, which approved it on December 24 (11), 1917.

By the Decree of February 2 (January 20), 1918, the school was separated from the church (see Document 35).

17. It was said in the resolution of the Petrograd Soviet of November 7 (October 25), 1917, which was drafted by Lenin, that the Soviet government would "establish national control over the banks, at the same time transforming them into a single state enterprise".

The banks met Soviet power with open sabotage. In response, on November 12 (October 30) the CPC gave orders to open the banks the next day at 10.00 a.m., and warned that in the event of disobedience the directors and members of the boards of the banks would be arrested. Commissars were sent to all banks. The sabotage of the bank employees hastened nationalization. On November 18 (5) Lenin announced in his appeal "To the Population" that the law on nationalization of the banks was being prepared. In the evening of December 27 (14) a decree was adopted. At all banks detachments of Soviet troops were posted.

At the Third Congress of Soviets Lenin said that the law on nationalization of the banks was one of the first measures of the Soviet Government aimed at undermining and eradicating the rule of capital.

In development of, and in addition to, the Decree on nationalization of banks, the ARCEC on the same day, December 27 (14), approved a decree on the inspection of strong boxes in the banks, according to which all money contained in the boxes was to be remitted to current accounts in the State Bank, and all gold confiscated. The Decree on the Annulment of State Loans (see Document 26) was passed on February 3 (January 21), 1918, the decree on the Confiscation of the Joint-Stock Capital of Former Private Banks on February 5 (January 25).

18. The Decree was drafted on the basis of recommendations worked out by the All-Army Committee at General Headquarters, and adopted by the CPC on December 28 (15), 1917. This and the following act (see Document 24) continued the democratization of the old army initiated by the decision of the Second All-Russia Congress of Soviets on the formation of provisional revolutionary committees in the army. The latter were charged with maintaining revolutionary order on the fronts and exercising control over the commanders-in-chief, who were subordinated to the committees.

19. This and the previous decree (see Document 23) were drafted on the basis of recommendations worked out by the All-Army Committee at General Headquarters, and adopted by the CPC on December 18 (15), 1917.

20. On January 28 (15), 1918, this Decree was endorsed by the Third All-Russia Congress of Soviets. On March 1, in Petrograd, a treaty concluded between the Russian and Finnish Socialist Republics. On behalf of the Soviet Government it was signed by V. I. Lenin, J. V. Stalin and P. P. Proshyan, and on behalf of the People's Commissioners of Finland, by E. G. Gülling and O. Tokoj. It was the first international treaty concluded by the Soviet Government.

21. The problem of wages confronted the Soviet Government from its very first days. The first legislative act in this field, adopted on December 1 (November 18), 1917, established a ceiling on the salaries of People's Commissars (500 roubles monthly) and instructed the People's Commissariat of Finance "to cut down all inordinately high salaries and pensions". This was followed by Government measures to raise the wages of the low-paid categories of factory and office workers: on December 18 (5)—a decision on issuing bonuses to the postal and telgraph workers; on December 24 (11)—a decree on wage rates for the railwaymen, setting the highest monthly wage at 510 roubles and the lowest at 155; on January 15 (2), 1918—the decision printed in this book; on April 1—a decree on rates for the People's Commissariat of State Control; on June 22—a decision on rates for teachers; on June 25—instructions on the order of endorsement of collective agreements specifying wage rates and working conditions (see Document 62); on June 27—a decree on wages and salaries for the employees of Soviet institutions, with monthly rates fixed between 350 and 800 roubles; the same decree allowed rates of up to 1,200 roubles for experts employed on special jobs and commissions.

22. On January 19 (6), 1918, Lenin submitted to the CPC his theses on the dissolution of the Constituent Assembly. The CPC accepted the theses and ordered a decree to be drafted on their basis and submitted to the ARCEC, with the recommendation "to suggest that the Central Executive Committee secure the participation in it, with the right of vote, of those groups in the Constituent Assembly which are prepared to cooperate with the Soviets". At 1.30 a.m. on January 20 (7) the decree was approved by the ARCEC.

The Constituent Assembly, convened by the Soviet Government, opened at the Taurida Palace in Petrograd on January 18 (5) 1918. The preparations for elections to it having been launched by the bourgeois Provisional Government of Kerensky, the composition of the Assembly reflected a past stage of the revolution and was not expressive of the new balance of political forces in the country. This explains why the Bolsheviks had received 25 per cent of the vote, the Mensheviks and Socialist-Revolutionaries 62 per cent, and the Constitutional-Democrats and other bourgeois parties 13 per cent. The majority of the Assembly was hostile towards Soviet power. Opening the Assembly, the ARCEC Chairman Sverdlov invited it to recognize Soviet power and its decrees, specifically, the Declaration of Rights of the Working and Exploited People. The counter-revolutionary majority rejected the proposal, whereupon the

Boshevik group headed by Lenin walked out of the sitting. Late at night it was followed by the Left-Wing Socialist-Revolutionaries, whose proposal on an immediate solution of the problems of land and peace had been turned down by the Assembly. Shortly afterwards P. Y. Dybenko, People's Commissar for the Navy who was in charge of security at the Taurida Palace, ordered the guard to close the sitting. The Constituent Assembly sitting was discontinued at 4.00 a.m. on January 19 (6).

23. The draft of this first constitutional act of Soviet power was written by Lenin and was to have been endorsed by the Constituent Assembly. Two days before the opening of the Assembly, the Declaration was approved by the ARCEC. The counter-revolutionary majority of the Constituent Assembly refused to place the Declaration on the agenda. In a somewhat revised form the Declaration was laid by the ARCEC Presidium before the Third All-Russia Congress of Soviets, which endorsed it on January 25 (12). Subsequently it was fully incorporated in the first Constitution of the RSFSR (see Document 64).

The Third All-Russia Congress of Soviets was held in Petrograd on January 23–31 (10–18), 1918. The first sitting was attended by 707 delegates, 441 of them Bolsheviks. On January 26 (13) the Third All-Russia Congress of Peasants' Deputies fully sided with it. At the last sittings, when most of the delegates had arrived, attendance reached 1,587. The Congress discussed reports by the ARCEC Chairman Y. M. Sverdlov and the CPC Chairman V. I. Lenin, and passed resolutions unreservedly supporting the policy of the ARCEC Chairman Y. M. Sverdlov and the CPC Chairman V. I. Lenin, and passed resolutions unreservedly supporting the policy of the ARCEC and the CPC and granting them full confidence. The Congress also heard a report by J. V. Stalin, People's Commissar for the Affairs of Nationalities, on the fundamentals of the federative arrangement of the Soviet republics. The Congress approved the Declaration of Rights of the Working and Exploited People (see Document 29) and adopted the Resolution on Peace (Document 31), the Resolution on the Fundamentals of the Constitution of the RSFSR (see Document 32), the Resolution Endorsing the Nationalities Policy of the Soviet Government (see Document 33), the Appeal to the Working Cossacks and, on the last day, on Lenin's proposal, a decree expunging all references to the Constituent Assembly from decrees and laws. The Congress also approved the basic principles of the law on the Socialization of land.

A new All-Russia Central Executive Committee was elected; 160 of its 306 members were Bolsheviks.

Taking the floor before the closing of the Congress, Lenin stressed that the Congress had consolidated the new State power created by the October Revolution and had "projected the lines for future socialist construction".

24. The question of war and peace was discussed by the Third Congress of Soviets on January 26 and 27 (13 and 14), 1918. The Bolsheviks and the Left-Wing Socialist-Revolutionaries moved separate draft resolutions, both of which were approved.

25. On January 28 (15), 1918, J. V. Stalin submitted to the Third Congress of Soviets a draft resolution on the federal institutions of the RSFSR, outlining the fundamentals of the Constitution. The resolution was passed with two amendments (Paragraphs 6 and 7) proposed by the Left-Wing Socialist-Revolutionaires.

26. It was announced in the Declaration of Rights of the Working and Exploited People that "the creation of a socialist Red Army of workers' and peasants . . . is hereby decreed" (see Document 29). Before being submitted to the Council of People's Commissars, the Decree on the Organization of the Red Army was thoroughly discussed at a meeting of the army delegates to the Third Congress of Soviets. On January 28 (15) the Decree was examined by the CPC, amended as proposed by Lenin, and approved.

Along with the Decree on the Organization of the Red Army, the CPC adopted a decree setting up, under the People's Commissariat for Military Affairs, an All-Russia Board for the formation of the Red Army, which was to provide guidance to local army-building establishments, keep record of newly-formed units, supervise unit formation and training, provide units with arms, all types of allowances and medical and sanitary assistance, work out manuals, instructions, etc. On January 29 (16) the CPC passed a decree appropriating 20 million roubles to organize the Red Army.

On May 29 the ARCEC issued a decision abolishing voluntary recruitment into the Red Army and decreeing transition to "general mobilization of workers and poorest peasants" (see Document 57).

27. The Decree was drafted by a special commission appointed by the CPC on December 24 (11), 1917. Lenin closely studied the draft and amended six paragraphs out of thirteen. On February 2 (January 20), 1918, the CPC approved the decree as amended by Lenin.

28. On April 18, 1918, in order to protect the interests of necessitous citizens, the Government issued a decree ordering registration of shares, bonds and other securities throughout Russia and abroad. Under the decree, the holders of bonds, including cancelled bonds, who registered them properly and in good time, retained the right to whatever was due to them on these bonds.

29. No central medical authority was established during the October Revolution. Its organization was preceded by the formation of local Soviet medical institutions. The Council of Medical Boards was the first step towards the creation of the People's Commissariat. The principal task of the Council was merely to coordinate the activities of the medical boards of People's Commissariats. Zemstvo and municipal medical establishments, factory and public organizations concerned with medical service, and Red Cross societies remained outside its competence. The unification of all the medical establishments of the country was launched by the People's Commissariat for Public Health instituted by the CPC decree of July 11, 1918.

30. Following the calendar reform, a start was made to prepare the introduction of time reckoning according to the international system of time zones. On May 1, 1918, the CPC decreed transition to this system for ships at sea; eleven months later, on April 1, 1919, this system was introduced throughout the RSFSR. On February 8, 1919, the CPC issued a decree dividing the territory of the Republic into eleven time zones.

31. Labour exchanges existed till the end of 1918. Under the Labour Code published on December 26–31, 1918, all matters of employment became the responsibility of the manpower distribution departments of local Soviets.

Concentrated in the Labour Code were all the relevant legislative acts issued in 1917 and 1918. It contained provisions regarding labour conscription, the right to hire workers, the procedure for hiring, probation, transfer, dismissal, remuneration, labour protection, ascertaining incapacity for work, payment of sickness benefits, payment of unemployment benefits, service records, weekly rest, and holidays.

32. Together with the decree on the organization of the Workers' and Peasants' Red Navy, regulations were issued according to which enlistment in the navy, as well as in the army, was to be voluntary. The new system became effective in the navy on February 14 (1), 1918. A model contract on volunteer service, contractual duties and rights of servicement, and pay rates were also published.

33. Lenin twice amended the draft of this Decree. On January 28 (15), 1918, he amended eight paragraphs, and on the same day the amendments were approved by the CPC. The second version of the draft, elaborated in the People's Commissariat for Justice, was amended by Lenin on February 12 (January 30). This time he corrected and supplemented six paragraphs. This version, amended and supplemented, was approved by the CPC and printed in the Government newspapers on February 20–21.

34. Written by Lenin, the Decree was adopted by the CPC on February 21, 1918, and the next day published in *Pravda* and *Izvestia*. It also appeared in leaflet form.

The decree was enacted in connection with the offensive which the German troops launched on February 18. The pretext the German command used to disrupt the talks was L. Trotsky's refusal to sign the peace treaty. At 19.30 on February 16 the Germans told the Soviet representatives at Brest-Litovsk that at noon on February 18 the armistice between Germany and Russia would be terminated and the state of war resumed. In the early hours of February 19 the Soviet Government sent a protest to the Government of the German Empire against the violation of the armistice of December 15 (2), 1917, and the resumption of hostilities by Germany, and declared "its readiness formally to conclude peace on the terms the German Government demanded at Brest-Litovsk". But the German Government was in no hurry to reply. Its troops continued to advance into Russia, seizing a number of towns and beginning to threaten Petrograd. Such was the situation when the Decree in question was issued. It was only on February 22 that the reply was handed to the Soviet courier. It contained new, even harder terms of peace and an ultimatum that these be considered within 48 hours. The reply was delivered to Petrograd in the morning of February 23, and on February 24 the CPC adopted, on Lenin's proposal, the following resolution: "In keeping with the decision adopted by the Central Executive Committee of Soviets of Workers', Soldiers' and Peasants' Deputies at 4.30 a.m. on February 24, the Council of People's Commissars has resolved to accept the terms of peace advanced by the German Government and to dispatch a delegation to Brest-Litovsk." At 7.32 a.m. the text of the resolution was transmitted to Berlin by the Tsarskoye Selo radio station. On March 3, 1918, the peace treaty between German and Russia was signed, and on March 15 it was ratified by the Extraordinary Fourth Congress of Soviets (see Document 44).

35. The resolution ratifying the Peace Treaty of Brest-Litovsk was

passed by the Extraordinary Fourth Congress of Soviets on March 15, 1918.

The Congress, convened to decide the question of ratification of that treaty, was held in Moscow on March 14–16, 1918. It was attended by 1,232 delegates, among them 795 Bolsheviks, 283 Left-Wing Socialist-Revolutionaries, 21 Mensheviks, and others. On behalf of the ARCEC, Lenin delivered a report peace. The Left-Wing Socialist-Revolutionaries B.. D. Kamkov spoke against ratification of the treaty. He was supported by the Mensheviks, Right-Wing Socialist-Revolutionaries, Maximalists, Anarchists and other representatives of petty-bourgeois parties. After sharp debates the overwhelming majority of the Congress carried, by a roll-call vote, the resolution on ratification of the peace treaty tabled by Lenin. 784 delegates voted for it, 261 against, and 115 abstained. The decision of the Congress was supported by the local Soviets, the Bolshevik Party organizations, and at public meetings.

The Congress also adopted a resolution concerning the message of President Wilson of the United States (March 14) and a decision to transfer the capital from Petrograd to Moscow (March 16).

After the Congress, by way of protest against the ratification of the peace treaty, the Left-Wing Socialist-Revolutionaries withdrew from the Council of People's Commissars.

36. On March 27, 1918, the CPC examined the draft Decree and referred it to the ARCEC as coming within the latter's competence. On April 1 the ARCEC approved the draft and forwarded it for final wording to its Presidium, which endorsed it on April 3.

37. The Second All-Ukraine Congress of Soviets, which opened on March 17, 1918, adopted a resolution by which the Ukraine was proclaimed an independent republic, closely linked by bonds of federation with the RSFSR. After the Congress a plenipotentiary embassy was sent to Moscow. On April 1 it was received at a sitting of the ARCEC, and on April 3 at a sitting of the CPC. The Council of People's Commissars unanimously recognized the Ukrainian Soviet Government and adopted the resolution printed here.

38. The question of cooperatives as a means of supplying the population with foodstuffs and other prime necessities preoccupied Lenin from the first days of the October Revolution. In December 1917 he wrote: "In order to ensure proper accounting and distribution of food and other necessities, every citizen of the States shall be obliged to join a consumers' society." This idea was amplified in the draft decree on consumers' communes written by Lenin on January

6–9, 1918 (December 24–27, 1917) and worked out in detail by the People's Commissariat for Food Supply. Printed in *Izvestia* on February 1 (January 19), the draft, particularly its stipulations regarding the nationalization of consumers' societies and the participation of the entire population in cooperatives, was vehemently objected to by the bourgeois cooperators. In its original form, the decree would have deprived the propertied strata of free control over cooperative property and of the possibility of using the cooperatives in their self-seeking interests, and afford the broad masses access to consumers' societies. In this situation the Government decided upon a compromise. Talks took place in March–April. On March 21, 1918, the Supreme Economic Council and representatives of the cooperatives reached an initial agreement, but at the Council's sitting on March 25, in which Lenin took part, the agreement was revised. On March 29, a conference of representatives of the SEC, cooperatives and supply agencies worked out a compromise draft which the Council of People's Commissars examined on April 9. On April 10 this draft, heavily amended by Lenin, was adopted by the CPC and the next day endorsed by the ARCEC. The latter's resolution on it pointed out that the Decree, "worked out on the basis of talks between representatives of the central cooperative organizations and the Council of People's Commissars . . . is a compromise solution having serious shortcomings", in view of which the ARCEC regarded it "as a transitional measure".

In his work, "The Immediate Tasks of the Soviet Government", Lenin pointed out that the decree was "an agreement with the bourgeois cooperative societies and the workers' cooperative societies which still adhere to the bourgeois point of view".

Later on, with a view to establishing a unified network of supply agencies, private trading establishments were abolished (the decree of November 21, 1918), and on March 16, 1919, a Decree on consumers' cooperatives was issued, setting up a single supply mechanism of which cooperative organizations constituted the basis.

39. The decision, adopted by the CPC on April 12 on the proposal of the People's Commissar for Public Education, A. V. Lunacharsky, is closely connected with Lenin's "Draft Plan of Scientific and Technical Work", in which Lenin proposed that the Supreme Economic Council instruct the Academy of Sciences to set up a number of commissions to elaborate problems of reorganizing industry and ensuring Russia's economic advancement: rational distribution of industry from the viewpoint of proximity to raw materials and the lowest consumption of labour power in the

transition from processing to the output of the finished product; rational merging and concentration of production in a few large enterprises; seeking ways of ensuring the country's self-sufficiency in all principal kinds of raw materials and main industries; special attention to the electrification of industry, transport and agriculture and wide use for these purposes of low-grade fuels, water power, and wind engines.

40. The decree was passed at a CPC sitting on April 12 on A. V. Lunacharsky's proposal. Attaching great importance to it, Lenin never lost sight of it and demanded of Lunacharsky its speediest implementation. On Lenin's initiative the CPC again discussed this question on July 8 and decided to appoint "a person to be responsible for energetic enforcement of the decree and its immediate implementation in Moscow". On July 17, in following up this decision, the CPC ruled that fifty monuments be erected in Moscow in memory of great revolutionaries, public leaders, philosophers, writers, scientists and artists, and a bas-relief be installed on the Kremlin wall opposite the graves of heroes of the October Revolution. On July 30 the CPC approved the list of monuments. Thirty-one of them were to perpetuate the memory of revolutionaries and public leaders. The list was topped by Spartacus, followed by Brutus, Babeuf, Marx, Engels, Bebel, and others. Twenty monuments were to be dedicated to writers and poets, three to philosophers and scientists, seven to painters, three to composers and two to artists.

41. The draft of this Decree was adopted by the ARCEC on April 22 and referred for final editing to the ARCEC Presidium, which approved the final text on April 25. Simultaneously the ARCEC adopted a decree on the order of appointment to posts in the Red Army (from squad commander upwards), a decree on the term of service in the Red Army (the first paragraph of which read: "Every citizen voluntarily enlisting in the Red Army commits himself to serve in it for at least six months from the day of signing the contract") and the text of the solemn pledge for Red Army men.

42. On January 11, 1918 (December 29, 1917) the CPC imposed a ban on the import and export of goods without permission of the People's Commissariat for Trade and Industry. The nationalization of certain branches of the national economy put on the order of the day nationalization of foreign trade. Lenin wrote in "The Immediate Tasks of the Soviet Government" that it was necessary to "consolidate and improve the State monopolies (in grain, leather, etc.)

which have already been introduced, and by doing so, prepare for the State monopoly of foreign trade. Without this monopoly we shall not be able to free ourselves from foreign capital by paying 'tribute' ". The Decree was adopted on April 22 by the CPC, and on April 25 taken note of by the ARCEC Presidium. On April 23 it was published in the central newspapers.

43. This Decree was a sequel to the CPC Decree of December 8 (November 25), 1917, establishing state monopoly of agricultural machines and implements (see Document 15). Prior to its approval it was closely studied by Lenin, who amended article 7, rewriting the entire second paragraph.

44. Prior to the examination of this Decree by the CPC Lenin introduced amendments into Paragraphs 5, 6, 11 and 12. On April 24, 1918, the CPC approved the draft as amended by Lenin and referred it to the ARCEC. On April 25 the ARCEC adopted it in substance and forwarded it for final wording to its Presidium, which approved the final text on April 27.

45. On April 29, 1918, after discussing Lenin's report on the immediate tasks of the Soviet Government, the ARCEC instructed him to summarize the substance in brief theses. These went down in history as "Six Theses on the Immediate Tasks of the Soviet Government." On May 3 the theses, with slight amendments, were unanimously approved by the Central Committee of the Bolshevik Party, and on May 4 the ARCEC sent them out to the local Soviets in a circular letter.

46. The need to discuss the international situation had arisen in view of the worsening relations with Germany which demanded the handover to Finland of Ino, a fort on the border with Finland which covered, together with Kronstadt, the approaches to Petrograd, and also in connection with the continuing occupation of Murmansk by the British, despite repeated protests of the Soviet Government, and the preparation of an invasion deep into the country. Lenin addressed the joint session of the ARCEC and the Moscow Soviet with a detailed report on these problems.

47. The first law on mobilization was adopted on June 11, 1918, appearing the next day in *Izvestia* and *Pravda*. It concerned workers and peasants not exploiting the labour of others who resided in the Volga, Urals and West-Siberian military districts. On June 17 a Decree was approved on the call-up of workers born in 1896 and

1897 residing in Moscow and its suburbs, and on June 29 three Decrees were issued: on the call-up of workers of Moscow and its suburbs who had served in the artillery and the engineer troops; on the call-up of workers born in 1896 and 1897 residing in Petrograd and its suburbs; and on the procedure to be followed in calling up government employees and factory workers.

These measures were preceded by the establishment throughout the country, under a Decree issued on April 8, 1918, of *volost, uyezd, gubernia* and district military commissariats to deal with matters of registration, call-up, formation of units, military training of workers and peasants not employing hired labour, troop control and material supply.

On June 17 the CPC decreed an increase in the salaries of Red Army soldiers: to 150 roubles for unmarried soldiers and 250 roubles for those with families.

48. On January 17 (4), 1918, the CPC launched the reorganization of the Russian Red Cross Society, setting up for the purpose a committee composed of representatives of eight institutions and organizations. The property of the Society was nationalized. The reorganization over, it became necessary to determine the attitude of the Society to the International Red Cross Committee. On May 25, 1918, the managing department of the CPC convneed a conference with the participation of representatives of the International Committee, the Russian Red Cross Reorganization Committee and the Moscow POW Relief Committee. The conference worked out the draft of the decision printed here, which was approved by the CPC on May 30.

49. Before considering the Regulations the CPC had them discussed by the boards of the People's Commissariats for Labour, Justice and State Control and the All-Russia Council of Trade Unions. On June 12 the CPC approved the draft with amendments, including those suggested by Lenin, and, in final form, on June 14, 1918. On June 15 and 18 the Regulations were published in *Izvestia*.

50. On November 30 (17), 1917, the Soviet Government nationalized the first industrial enterprise: a mill belonging to A. V. Smirnov's Likinskaya Partnership in Vladimir Gubernia. On December 7 (November 24), in view of wholesale sabotage on the part of industrialists, the CPC adopted and sent out to local bodies a decision on the rights of local Soviets in the fight against saboteurs and on the rules of confiscation of their enterprises (see Document 14). Next came acts nationalizing, for refusal to abide by the decree

on workers' control, enterprises of the joint-stock companies of the Bogoslovsky mining district (December 20/7/), the Simsky mining district (December 22 /9/) and the Russo-Belgian Metallurgical Society (December 28/15/). In all, 52 nationalization acts were adopted by the Government. The Soviet Government started with individual enterprises but soon proceeded to nationalize whole branches: on February 5 (January 23), 1918, the merchant marine; on February 15, all grain-storages; on May 2, the sugar-refining industry; on June 20, the oil industry, and on June 28 enterprises listed in the Decree printed here. The right of further nationalization was then delegated to the Presidium of the Supreme Economic Council, which carried this work to completion.

51. On January 28 (15), 1918, the Third All-Russia Congress of Soviets adopted a decision on the fundamentals of the Constitution of the RSFSR, instructing the ARCEC to draft the Constitution and submit it to the next Congress (see Document 32). On April 1 the ARCEC ordered its Presidium to set up a drafting committee. On April 3 the Presidium approved the following composition of the drafting committee: three members from the Bolsheviks, two from the Left-Wing Socialist-Revolutionaries, one from the Maximalist Socialist-Revolutionaries and one from each of the Commissariats for Internal Affairs, Nationalities Affairs, Justice, Finance and Military Affairs and the Supreme Economic Council. At the first meeting of the committee, held on April 5, Sverdlov was elected its chairman. On April 8, the ARCEC approved the committee. Its work proceeded in keen struggle between the Bolsheviks on one side and the Left-Wing and Maximalist Socialist-Revolutionaries and the Anarcho-Syndicalists, on the other. The draft was ready in time for the opening of the Fifth All-Russia Congress of Soviets. A number of corrections in its text had been made by Lenin.

At its first sitting on July 4, 1918, the Fifth Congress elected, on Sverdlov's proposal, a constitution commission of six full and three alternate members. On Lenin's proposal, the commission included in the Constitution the Declaration of Rights of the Working and Exploited People. The commission also added to it the parts "Budgetary Law" and "The Emblem and the Flag of the RSFSR". At its last session on July 10, the Congress unanimously adopted the Constitution, instructing the ARCEC to finalize its wording and put it in force. On July 18 the ARCEC Presidium approved the final text of the Constitution and resolved to have it translated into all languages and printed on good paper.

V. I. Lenin said about the first Constitution of the RSFSR: "There have never been constitutions in the world such as ours.

In it is recorded the experience of struggle and organization of proletarian masses against exploiters both inside the country and throughout the world."

The Fifth All-Russia Congress of Soviets was held in Moscow's Bolshoi Theatre on July 4–10, 1918. It was attended by 1,164 delegates with the right to vote, among them 773 Bolsheviks, 353 Left-Wing Socialist-Revolutionaries, 17 Maximalists, four Anarchists and 17 representatives of other parties and non-party delegates.

Sverdlov reported on the activities of the ARCEC, and Lenin, on the activities of the CPC. After heated debates the Congress carried, by a majority vote, the Bolshevik resolution expressing "complete approval of the foreign and domestic policy of the Soviet Government". The Left-Wing Socialist-Revolutionaries tabled their own resolution, insisting on a no-confidence vote, denunciation of the Peace Treaty of Brest-Litovsk, and a reorientation of foreign and domestic policy. Their resolution was rejected. Defeated at the Congress, the Left-Wing Socialist-Revolutionaries resolved upon an open armed insurrection, which they launched on July 6. The Congress adjourned and did not resume until July 9. After hearing the Government's report on the events of July 6–7, it fully approved the resolute measures that had been taken to put an end to the Left-Wing Socialist-Revolutionaries' criminal adventure, and stressed that those of them who shared the views of their leaders "shall have no place in the Soviets of Workers' and Peasants' Deputies".

The Congress adopted the following documents: a resolution on the struggle against provocateurs in Red Army units on the Ukrainian front (July 4); a message of greetings to Russian prisoners-of-war abroad (July 4); a message of greetings to Russian soldiers in France (July 4); a resolution on the reports of the ARCEC and the CPC (July 5); a decision in connection with the assassination of the German Ambassador and the insurrection of the Left-Wing Socialist-Revolutionaries in Moscow (July 9); a decision on organization of the Red Army (July 10), and the Constitution of the RSFSR (July 10).